C000247137

LETTER FROM REACHFAR

By *Jane Duncan*

MY FRIENDS THE MISS BOYDS
MY FRIEND MURIEL
MY FRIEND MONICA
MY FRIEND ANNIE
MY FRIEND SANDY
MY FRIEND MARTHA'S AUNT
MY FRIEND FLORA
MY FRIEND MADAME ZORA
MY FRIEND ROSE
MY FRIEND COUSIN EMMIE
MY FRIENDS THE MRS MILLERS
MY FRIENDS FROM CAIRNTON
MY FRIEND MY FATHER
MY FRIENDS THE MACLEANS
MY FRIENDS THE HUNGRY GENERATION
MY FRIEND THE SWALLOW
MY FRIEND SASHIE
MY FRIENDS THE MISSES KINDNESS

as *Janet Sandison*

JEAN IN THE MORNING
JEAN AT NIGHT
JEAN IN THE TWILIGHT
JEAN TOWARDS ANOTHER DAY

for *children*

CAMERONS AHOY
CAMERONS AT THE CASTLE
CAMERONS CALLING
CAMERONS ON THE HILLS
CAMERONS ON THE TRAIN

for *younger children*

HERSELF AND JANET REACHFAR

LETTER FROM
REACHFAR

Jane Duncan.

M

© Jane Duncan 1975

All rights reserved. No part of this publication may be reproduced or transmitted, in any form or by any means, without permission.

SBN: 333 18755 5

First published 1975 by
MACMILLAN LONDON LTD
London and Basingstoke
Associated companies in New York
Dublin Melbourne Johannesburg and Delhi

Printed in Great Britain by
Northumberland Press Ltd
Gateshead

The passages from Vincent van Gogh's letters in Chapter 7 are quoted from *Dear Theo*, edited by Irving Stone and Jean Stone (Constable, 1937).

The photograph of George Cameron at Jemimaville is by Ursula Powys, A.I.B.P.

Dear Editor,

When you visited me here a few weeks ago, you suggested that I should record my part in the war against Nazism and Fascism as a photographic interpreter in the Women's Auxiliary Air Force. Because I try, despite my tendency to argue, to do in the end what you ask of me, I tried to write the book you suggested but in trying I discovered that the years of the war were some of the most sterile of my life and that there was very little in those years that I wished to record. The little that I consider to be of any value is contained in the pages that follow.

The attempt to do what you asked 'took off' for me, however, into something completely different, something that I really wanted to say and have wanted to say for a long time to you and my other readers. As you know, quite a number of readers are sufficiently interested in my novels to write to me and the question that is most frequently asked is: 'Are your books autobiographical?'

I thought it might be of interest if I sketched the background of my life and placed the novels against it, in an endeavour to show how fiction arises out of fact by some mysterious process that I cannot explain.

You also know that I have been asked to speak of books and the writing of them at a variety of gatherings and I have used some of the questions that I have been asked as headings for the following chapters. After each question, I have given my brief answer and the chapters themselves are a development of these answers.

I know that you will read what I have written with the care you give to everything I write and if you think it is of interest, perhaps it will make a book that answers some of the questions that my readers ask.

Yours,
Jane

Chapter 1

How did you get your first book published?
I was blown in on a Side Wind.

Dear Readers, as many of you know, I have taken, during the last year or two, to sending out printed cards in acknowledgement of the letters you write to me, instead of replying personally as I used to do. I took this step mainly to save time, but I must also admit that the writing of personal replies was very boring, because so many of you asked the same questions. This does not imply that the letters I received were boring – far from it – for what you told me of yourselves was always of interest. It was having to reply about myself that was the bore.

So, when I made the decision to have the cards printed, I made this other decision that, one day when time permitted, I would try to write a longish letter which would attempt to answer the many questions you have asked me. This letter, therefore, promises to be a discursive rambling thing, not an autobiography of the sixty-four years I have lived through. Indeed, I think that autobiography is an art far beyond my powers, an art far beyond the powers of most people, for it is given to very few to see themselves clearly, warts and all.

I write to you from my home, which is in a tiny village in Ross-shire in the Highlands of Scotland. I have warned you of discursions and here is one for there is something that I think is of interest about this village – two things, in fact.

About a mile from our post office which is also the village shop, there is a large, rather beautiful old house called Poyntzfield. This is an extraordinary name for a Highland house and it is said to have originated in this way. In the eighteenth century, the house and estate were called Ardoch, a much more likely name for this part of the country, and Ardoch was inherited by that not unusual creature in Scottish social history, a penniless lad wi' a lang pedigree who, like many more of his kind, went south to find himself a wealthy bride. He found her in Suffolk – some say in Norfolk – and her name was Jemima

1

Poyntz, for she was the daughter of a Dutch father and an English mother. Having brought her from these lush lands to the Highlands, the young laird of Ardoch made additions to the house with her dowry, in the form of two wings added to the bare rectangular block which made a pretty three-sided courtyard, and at the back of the original block he added a tower with an onion-shaped roof. The effect of these additions is curiously Dutch or perhaps merely foreign to Ross-shire. Then, in further compliment to his bride, he renamed both house and estate Poyntzfield but this was not all. He went on to build a row of cottages for his workers on the north seaward boundary of the estate and this has grown into the village of some twenty-five houses which bears the name of Jemimaville, where I now live. Miss Jemima Poyntz, if this story is true, and it is fairly well documented, is well commemorated.

The other thing about our village which I find interesting is its postal service. I have read that, as early as 1661, there was some form of postal service in Britain which used hand-struck stamps but I think it unlikely that there would be a postal service in remote Ross-shire until much later and when the service did come to this area, it took the form of a 'Postal Ride', a man on a horse who brought incoming letters and took away outgoing ones and the clearing-house or what we would nowadays call the post office for this activity in this area was the 'big house' of Poyntzfield, the home of the local laird and he had a postal frank which bore the name of his house. Later, a post office as we know it today was established in the village of Jemimaville but, whether out of petty economy or through an oversight, the frank was moved from big house to village without alteration which leads to the fact that this village is one of the few, if not the only one, in Britain that has a postal frank bearing a name different from that of the village in which the post office is situated. On the map, this is Jemimaville but postally this is Poyntzfield. Interesting?

And what, you may want to ask, has the postal service to do with the life of a writer? And I shall answer that the postal service had and still has much to do with my life.

From quite an early age, I had the desire to write, and down the years covered many a sheet of paper with words, but from my files I see that the important moment came in April 1957, when I wrote a short letter to a firm of literary agents in London, asking them if they would give me an opinion on a novel I had written. The postal service carried this letter from the West Indies, some four thousand miles away.

In common with most writers, I think, I had always read and still do read a great deal and I have the reader's inability to pass a bookshop without going in and spending as much as I can afford. I had been on holiday in Britain in 1956, had entered a bookshop and because of the latent writer in me, I suppose, I had bought a copy of a publication entitled: *The Writers' and Artists' Year Book*. It was from this, by taking a stab at a page with a darning-needle, that I found the address of the agents. These people replied politely to my letter and on 27th May I committed the typescript of *My Friend Muriel* to the postal service but heard no more until early September, when I received a rather discouraging letter to the effect that the agents' readers thought the novel '– despite its qualities, would be difficult to place'. Nevertheless, the agents decided to try it on a publisher who refused it, although one of his readers compared it 'not unfavourably' with Stevie Smith's *Novel on Yellow Paper*. In this letter, on the advice of this refusing publisher, the agents made some tentative suggestions about 'alterations' to the script and I wrote back, rather tersely: '– but do, if you can at all, avoid the "alteration" business. I do not want to tear the structure apart if I can possibly help it.'

The script was now sent to a second publisher whose judgement remains unknown for now an extraordinary thing happened. The writing world is not made up entirely of authors and publishers. It embraces a great number of people who have a great love for books and one of these was a reader for this second firm of publishers and a reader, of course, does not read for only one firm. It was my good fortune that this reader, a lady of tremendous enthusiasm, liked my book enough to mention it to the fiction editor of another firm, but I discovered this and thanked her for her interest only many months later. In September of 1957, what the agents wrote was: '– and we now have an enquiry for it from Macmillan, who have somehow heard of it by a side wind', which explains why I always think of this pretty, vivacious, enthusiastic lady reader as 'The Side Wind'. Early in January of 1958, the agents wrote again: 'Although I have not had a formal suggestion of terms from Macmillan, who have your book under consideration at the moment, I have had their Editor there on the telephone to say that they will be making me an offer early in the New Year.' Later in January, the agent wrote giving details of the offer and saying: 'I am delighted to have had a firm offer for what I think is a most unusual and excellent book—' I am afraid that I did not care whether the book was considered to be unusual or excellent. All I cared about was that my toe was on the lowest rung of the ladder and all I worried about – and I worried a great deal – was that I would be allowed to write in my own way and not be forced into too many 'alterations'.

There were a few very minor alterations to *My Friend Muriel*. In the original script, every other page contained the words 'Dear Reader' because I had always liked this old-fashioned direct approach to the reader and I thought it conveyed the thought behind my writing. I write as a friend to a friend who is my dear reader. This is the only way I can write.

However, we have to remember that, in 1958, *My Friend Muriel* was an 'unusual' book and by way of making it more 'usual' I suppose, I was asked to delete the recurrent phrase and I tried to do as I was asked. But if one does a thing unwillingly, it seems, one automatically does it badly and it will be found that in the published version of the book, there are no fewer than six 'dear readers' glaring up from the printed pages. I make no apology for this. Indeed, I am glad that I got away with them, for the words remain sincere. I have told in some detail of the acceptance of my first novel to try to dispel a firmly-rooted idea that the writing world is a closed shop where, in order to achieve publication, a writer has to be in the know or have influence. At the time of the acceptance of *My Friend Muriel*, I was a housewife who had no connections whatsoever with the world of writing, and living four thousand miles away from London, the centre of British publishing. In the forty-seven years of my life at that time, I had met only one writer, George Orwell, who terrified me out of my wits. He said 'How d'you do?' to me, gave me a piercing glance of what felt like utter disdain and walked away to sit in a greenhouse among some unripe tomatoes. I also want to pay tribute to the Side Wind. Since that time, I have discovered that there are many of them in the writing world, people who work with a devotion beyond the call of mere duty to help even a very minor talent on its way. Their devotion is only secondary to the talent. It is

4

given first to the Word, the Book and any small talent that can contribute in the slightest way to their devoted belief in the written word becomes the object of their care. The Side Wind had nothing to gain from her enthusiasm except, perhaps, the satisfaction that what she believed to be a talent, however slight, was given a chance.

It was thus, then, that I entered the world of writing and by coincidence the post brought me the formal contract with the publishers on the morning of my forty-eighth birthday. An association was formed at that time which has remained for all of us, I think, pleasant and rewarding until the present day. It seems to be a fact of life, though, that moments of unclouded happiness are very rare. At the time of the arrival of the contract, my husband who had been an invalid for some five years, was seriously ill and six weeks later, he died. It was like the closing of one door and the opening of another into the strange new world of writing and publishing which I found very frightening, alone as I was four thousand miles from home, with very little money and an 'unusual' book going into print which might fail utterly to justify even the advance of one hundred pounds which the signing of the contract had brought me. I went through a period of terrifying indecision and uncertainty of which I remember very little, between the months of March and June, but I discover from copies of letters of that time that, in June, I went to stay on a plantation in the hills where a friend turned over to me a large many-windowed room in her beautiful old house.

When I wrote to my editor, to tell him of my change of address and describing this room, he said in the course of his reply: 'From your description it could be the haven which most good writers have complained for years about not having.' At that time I too thought that I had found the ideal writing place but I have since recognised that the few months I spent there were very sterile. In that ideal haven, I did not produce one sentence that I have retained in my published work.

Fortunately, this did not matter for, although I later destroyed all that I wrote when there, I had in my possession the manuscripts of six more novels and *My Friend Monica* was despatched to London, followed in July by *My Friend Rose* and what was known at that time as *My Friends The Misses Boyd*. The postal service between London and my room on the green hill above the village of Runaway Bay and the Caribbean became very busy and believe it or not, one of the things that niggled at me about that ideal haven was the postal address 'Runaway Bay'. Every time I opened an envelope that bore this address, I suffered a faint queasy qualm in the pit of my stomach. Why was I not going home to my own country? Was I running away, afraid to face these publishing people in London?

In the realm of fact, if it is of any interest, Runaway Bay is so named because it was reputed to be the place from which the Spaniards ran away finally when the island was taken over by the British, but I have a mind that bends and fictionalises facts and sees in them significances which are peculiar to itself so that this name, for me, had little connection with the tradition of runaway Spaniards.

However, I ignored the qualms and the address for most of the time and got on with my typing. When *My Friends The Misses Boyd* arrived in London, the transatlantic postal service really began to hum. By this time, *My Friend Muriel* was being set up at the printers with a view to publication early in 1959, the first slight alterations to *My Friend Monica* were in train and now, in September of 1958, my editor wrote: 'We feel very strongly that we should publish *My Friends The Misses Boyd* first.'

The suggestion did not please me in the very least and I said so with great vehemence in a letter of enormous length. It shames me now to think of the letters I inflicted on that editor and it amazes me when I remember them that he even speaks to me now, much less regards me as a friend. To demonstrate the enormity of my shameless ego, I shall quote here a single paragraph of my reply to this first letter suggesting that *My Friends The Misses Boyd* should lead the series of novels.

'The ultimate aim of the books as a group is not so much to tell a series of stories as to delineate the development of a woman called Janet Sandison – she is the heroine as well as the narrator. I wished the development of her character to become apparent in the mind of the reader as if that reader had met Janet and had learned about her by hearing these stories from her own lips. Therefore, most readers of novels being over twenty years of age, I wanted them to meet first an adult woman, a woman in middle life, to wit, Janet, aged 37, as she is at the end of *My Friend Muriel*. Having met her in *My Friend Muriel*, the reader who finds her interesting is given in the subsequent novels the opportunity to learn more about her by hearing her tell another story about her friend Monica, sees at the same time a new stage in Janet's development and begins to hear a very little about her childhood in the north of Scotland; then in the story of Rose, the reader is taken back to a different stage in Janet's life and a little more of the earlier background is filled in. This, it seems to me, is how people come to know one another in life. At the *fourth* story, the *Misses Boyd*, Janet feels that the friendship between her and the reader is such that she can tell this story of her early childhood and, incidentally, having told the reader of that part of her life, she gains the confidence to tell of her difficult and unhappy adolescence which is the subject of the fifth book, *My Friend Annie*.'

In reply to the diatribe of which the above quotation is about one tenth, my editor took the pains to write a reply almost as long in which he gave cogent reasons for the alteration in order and this letter ends: 'I therefore beg you to put your tiny paw in ours and let us go forward with *The Miss Boyds*. PS. Incidentally, don't you think *My Fs the Miss Boyds* wd be slightly better than *My Fs the Misses Boyd*?'

In reply to this, I wrote in my ungracious way:

'Dear Editor,

If I had ever met you, this letter would read: Publish the confounded things in any order you darn please and stop bothering me, but as I know you only by letter and one should try to be moderately polite in letters, please go ahead with the *Boyds* and call it *My Friends the Miss Boyds* too and if the customers decide that I am illiterate, I shall be able to say that it is all your fault.... I feel that your reference to my tiny paw could not be more apt – I feel a little like a mechanical monkey on a stick.... However the tiny paw is now in yours and has every confidence that it will be led in the right direction.'

I did not at this time see that the reference to the tiny paw was his recognition of the fact that, in relation to the publishing world, I was a child who had to be led. Looking back to those early days of mine in this writing world, I can only conclude that there is a Providence which provides editors to guide those fools who are called writers.

This argument over the order of publication and the patience and understanding I had been shown were, I think, a large factor in the next decision I made. The many letters that had been exchanged between my editor, my agent and me since I had written that first letter to the agency in April, 1957 had made me feel that I had a nucleus of new friends in London and that I had found a way of going forward into a new life.

I had been in the West Indies for ten years, broken by short home leaves at longish intervals and ten years was long enough for me to lose track of everybody I had known except the members of my immediate family. This consisted of my brother, my sister-in-law, their four children and my Uncle George, who was now in his late seventies and lived alone in a little cottage here in Jemimaville. Quite suddenly, in November 1958, I wrote to my editor: 'You are in for a shock. I have decided to come back to Britain and take up residence with my uncle in the north of Scotland.'

This was easy to write but the practical undertaking was a different matter for, although I had sold many of my household possessions, I still had furniture, linen, china and books that I did not want to part with but, somehow, I bought wood, had crates made and had them shipped to the port. I booked a passage in a ship, my editor booked me into a hotel in London; the ship cancelled her sailing, I booked in another ship, feeling that I was tempting the Fates of the ocean (My Friends The Misses Kindness?) and eventually sailed on 23 December, whereupon the Atlantic rose in such fury that I thought it would drown the ship and all of us on board. A seaman was lost overboard in the course of the voyage.

This ship, SS *Essequibo*, had accommodation for twelve passengers but was carrying only five, who were a Syrian couple travelling on their honeymoon, an Englishman of the Jamaican Prison Service going home on leave, an elderly spinster and myself. Naturally enough, we saw little of the honeymoon couple and the Prison Officer preferred the company of the ship's officers so that the elderly spinster and I were automatically thrown on the mercy of one another. She was rather a sad old lady who had emigrated to the West Indies to spend her retirement there but had been disappointed in the way of life she found and was now making a dreary seasick journey home again. I tell you about her at all because of one extraordinary thing. So here is what will look at first like a pointless digression.

Publishers' readers and some reviewers of whom, now, I have a fair amount of experience, have an attitude to coincidence that is almost a phobia. 'That coincidence just won't *do!*' they say in tones of near terror. 'Nobody would *believe* it!' But I have found coincidence in real life only too common and one is given no choice as to believing it or not. It is simply there, as an incontrovertible fact.

Those of you who remember *My Friend Muriel* may also remember that she had a habit of entering all the money she spent in a blue notebook. Well, this old lady and I disembarked from SS *Essequibo* at Liverpool on a cold morning of early January in 1959 and decided to have lunch at a hotel while waiting for the London train. As soon as we were seated in the railway carriage, she took from her handbag a blue notebook, copied into it the total of her luncheon bill, then said as she wrote: 'And two shillings to the porter.' She then put the notebook back in her bag, looked across at me and said: 'My dear, I feel I know you after all these stormy days at sea. You must call me by my first name. It is Muriel.'

I would remind you that, at this time, my novel *My Friend Muriel* was being set up in type in London and I assure you that I had not met this lady until twelve days before, when I joined the ship.

Chapter 2

When did you first start to write?
Ce sont les lapins qui ont été étonnés!
(It was the rabbits who were astonished!)

ALPHONSE DAUDET.

At the age of twelve, I entered the Second Year of the upper school at my good, sound Scottish academy. At this time, my favourite subject was French, which I had begun to learn the year before. The reasons for this preference were, I think, that I liked the language for itself, for its musical fluidity and I liked the mistress who taught it, a dignified lady of great culture, (Edinburgh University and the Sorbonne) as academy mistresses were in those days, who seemed to be able to impart some of her own love of the language to her pupils. The first year of study had been given mainly to vocabulary and grammar. Those were still the days of the 'pen of my aunt' mode of teaching but in spite of this, I never found the lessons dull and I was delighted when, at the beginning of this second year, I was given an actual *book* in French that could be read, along with a dictionary that would help one through the puzzling parts. The book was *Lettres de mon Moulin* by Alphonse Daudet, a collection of short articles and stories sent from the Provençal windmill he had bought to a Paris newspaper and the first little article opens with the words: 'Ce sont les lapins qui ont été étonnés!' I had to look up the word 'lapins' in my dictionary, for rabbits had not figured in my lessons of the year before and when I had gathered the meaning of the sentence I, as well as the rabbits, was astonished.

'Just imagine', I thought, 'anybody writing about rabbits!'

I had been able to read English since the age of three and was 'the nose always in a book' sort of child but most of the reading matter that came my way had been fairy tales, stories of children who lived in nurseries and had a background very different from my own, *Alice's Adventures in Wonderland* which I disbelieved profoundly and which yet terrified me and a few late Victorian and Edwardian novels of high moral tone. In addition to such fiction, we had in our house a copy of *The Pilgrim's Progress*, a large bible bound in dark green boards, a *Chambers Dictionary* of similar size in similar boards and a fascinating eight volumes of *Mysteries of Police and Crime* also, oddly enough, of similar size to the Bible and in dark green boards. For quite a long time, my mother thought I was reading the Bible or the dictionary – I actually read large gobbets of the dictionary – in bed at nights only to discover eventually that I was immersed in the corpse-ridden story of Burke and Hare in a volume of *Mysteries of Police and Crime*, but to her credit she did not act as a censor and take the book away from me. These were the books of my 'away home'. There were other books at my 'real home' and we shall come to those later. The point I wish to make here is that when I read about the rabbits, I was in the ambience of my 'away home', where none of the books dealt in a discursive way with rabbits, creatures which were a familiar feature of my 'real home'.

The reason that we owned the eight volumes of *Mysteries of Police and Crime* was that my father was a policeman, which fact will probably be a disappointment to those of you who are convinced that the Reachfar series of novels is totally autobiographical. Later on, I hope to deal with the subject of autobiography but at the moment I shall make a short digression to tell you of a little incident at the time when *My Friend My Father* was published. An old lady of this district – dead now unfortunately – was an avid reader of my books. She had known my family all her life and had known me almost since the day I was born, for I was brought home to this district on holiday for the first time, I have been told, at the age of three months. Her daughter had told her of the publication of *My Friend My Father* and was at once sent to Inverness to buy it. As the daughter made ready to go on the errand, the old lady said: 'Now, I wonder if it will be about her farmer-father or her policeman-father?' It is one of my few claims to distinction that I have been, even if for only a moment, thought to have had two fathers.

But, back to our rabbits. You will notice that the early reading at my 'away home' was all of high moral tone. The fairy stories ended happily ever after. The picture-book stories about the middle-class nursery children were mostly records of the comeuppance of naughtiness. *The Pilgrim's Progress* was all about the struggle to get to Heaven, all the people in the Bible were good just because they were in the Bible, the dictionary was a very serious affair of great learning and the *Mysteries of Police and Crime* showed very clearly what happened to people who were wicked. (My favourite story in all eight volumes was that of Jack the Ripper, the one who got away.) So, just imagine anybody writing about *rabbits* and getting away with it into solemn print! *I* could write about rabbits, I thought. I could write about rabbits darting into the Bluebell Bank at The Colony.

The Colony. This was my 'real home' as I called it in my mind. This was the origin of my fictional 'Reachfar'. It was the birthplace of my father and of many of my ancestors before him, a small croft on top of a hill in the Black Isle of Ross-shire, to which I was taken for my first holiday at three months old and where I spent all my holidays until I went to England to earn my living at the age of twenty-one.

It was called 'The Colony' I have been told because once upon a time a colony of weavers lived on that ground, who gradually died off and drifted away, leaving mine as the last surviving family who gradually took over the abandoned sixty acres of marginal arable and the hundred and fifty of moorland. I can remember the ruins of the last abandoned houses in some of our fields when I was a child. Just as The Colony had swallowed up the surrounding smaller crofts one by one, it has itself now been swallowed up by a bigger farm, but its name still remains on the Ordnance Survey map of the area.

The school terms of my life were lived in police stations, usually in the less salubrious environs of Glasgow, for it is in such places that there is the greatest need for police stations and as a policeman's child, I was always slightly suspect by my fairly lawless contemporaries. This apart, I do not think that I was a very friendly or sociable youngster, for I was an only child until I was ten years old. Quite early, I had turned The Colony into a fantasy world – not the people there but the place itself which was like a private country of the mind – of mental escape during school time and I returned to it in fact every holiday with great joy.

As a little sidelight on history, I first made the journey from Glasgow to Inverness by myself at the age of five in the summer of 1915. The reason for this was that at that time of the Great War, the Cromarty Firth was one of the main bases of the North Sea Fleet and was consequently a protected area. It was discovered that, to enter it, my mother would have to have a passport which would take some weeks to obtain, my father, who could have travelled on his police warrant, could not get leave from duty and I, released from my first term at school, was clamouring for The Colony, so my poor parents, in desperation, pinned a label with my name and address and a little money inside my coat and my father took me to Buchanan Street Station in Glasgow and put me in charge of the guard. I remember playing in the guard's van with a large black retriever dog but I do not remember being handed, as I am assured I was, sound asleep, from the arms of a large Australian soldier into those of my Uncle George at Inverness. I do remember, though, the enchanted moment when I jumped down from the trap to open the march gate of The Colony so that my uncle could drive the trap through into my conception of Paradise.

Now, back again to the rabbits. As I read, with the help of my dictionary, Daudet's *Letters from my Windmill*, I remained amazed and delighted. There was the story of M. Séguin's goat which reminded me of the goats that danced on the thatched roof of a croft near The Colony. There was the story of the Pope of Avignon's mule, a spiteful animal who retained his kick for seven years until the opportunity came to deliver it to the right person, a story that made me think of the many 'horse persons' at The Colony and on the farms round about. There was the story of the Curate of Cucugnan, so worried about the latter end of his parishioners, who said from his pulpit: 'I have charge of your souls and I wish, I *wish* to save you from the abyss to which you are rolling head first!' and who might have been the minister in the church at Cromarty who wanted so much to render us the service that the Curate wished to render his Cucugnanais.

In short, I had made what was, for me, the tremendous discovery that books could be written about 'ordinary' people like those I knew. Books did not have to be about fairies or children in nurseries with nannies. They did not, either, have to be factual reportage like *Mysteries of Police and Crime* or the more frightening reportage of the Old Testament on the prophets and the ways of their terrible God of Vengeance. This *Letters from my Windmill* was the most enjoyable book I had read to date and it was all about poor peasant people, very much like those at The Colony and all around it.

So, although at the age of twelve I did not think of putting pen to paper, I am convinced that it was at the age of twelve that I began to write. Those astonished rabbits stayed with me and from then on I could never see the white retreating scut of a rabbit without remembering Daudet's words as he described his arrival at his windmill: '– there were, without a word of a lie, a good twenty, sitting in a ring on the platform, busy warming their paws in a moonbeam.' It was a pretty picture and one that I had seen many times at various places on the lands of The Colony.

I encountered *Letters from my Windmill* in 1922 and I went on and up through school and on and up through university in the period now known sometimes as The Roaring Twenties, the time of the Bright Young Things, whose spokesman was Noël Coward, but I did not belong to this gilded group.

In the last years of this decade, I was reading English Literature and Language at Glasgow University and writing the literature of the time were E. M. Forster, Lewis Grassic Gibbon, Ernest Hemingway, D. H. Lawrence, James Joyce, W. B. Yeats and a good many more. Perhaps all that was being written was not, precisely, literature but the interesting thing was that at Glasgow University at that time, Literature was seen to have come to an end with Charles Dickens. The Faculty of English hinted in an uneasy murmur that somebody called Thomas Hardy had been vaguely heard of but decided not to do anything rash and certainly not to pay any attention to such foreigners as Nathaniel Hawthorne and Henry James.

However, some of us students read some of what was being written and naturally I remember the books that were most severely frowned upon. None of us had very much money but each of us contrived to contribute to the pool some frowned-upon contemporary work and I still have one of these contributions, *Death of a Hero*, a novel of the Great War by Richard Aldington, which was considered to deserve total banning by some of the pundits. Its pages are dotted with asterisks as in the following extract: 'Winterbourne listened and heard a dull hollow sound of coughing. "Fritz's sentry," whispered the man. "Pore old ****** needs some liquorice."' I quote this because what amazed me and my young literature-reading colleagues was that any publisher or any member of the Faculty of English should think that we were so deaf and generally unreceptive that we had been walking along the streets of Glasgow for two or three years and had never learned the word 'bugger' or uglier words that would require a similar or greater or lesser number of asterisks. We were, after all, students of English Literature and *Language*. If the adult world considered us to be thus dim-witted, we thought, it should not have admitted us to university at all.

It was a repressive form of education, to indulge in a contradiction in terms and the strong moral tone was still very evident. I remember having to write an essay on Milton's *Lycidas* and if I had been truthful about my opinion at that time, I would have written: 'Milton is a pompous old bore who cannot even think straight,' and have left it at that but my family wanted me to achieve a degree, didn't they? So I, who am endowed with a very retentive memory, wrote a panegyric on *Lycidas* along the lines of the lectures I had heard on the subject. Milton is good and right and enthroned as part of Literature, was the implication of the lectures, and don't any of you dare to say a word against him. This attitude was not calculated to instil any confidence in his taste or any attempt at critical judgement on the part of the student and I was to be hampered by this and other repressions for a long time.

On the whole, I think the most important things I learned from my reading of English Literature and Language were the words 'bore' and 'boredom'. They were words never used in my family circle and when I became aware of them I discovered that boredom was something that existed, apparently, but that it had never happened to me in my whole life.

Yet I spent a great deal of my time alone. I was extremely shy and made no close friends at the university, merely acquaintances with whom I swopped the frowned-upon books. I travelled about twenty miles from the current police station by bus or train to attend my classes and twenty miles home again afterwards and at home I was still, virtually, an only child. My brother had been born when I was ten but my mother had died shortly afterwards and Baby John had gone to The Colony, into the care of our grandparents and Uncle George. By the time I went to university, my father had re-married but I had little in common with my stepmother and my free time was spent either reading in my room or walking in the hills beyond the town. Yet, I repeat, I never suffered from boredom and at this late date I recognise that this was because the rabbits were always there, astonishing as ever. I still had not put pen to paper because I could not find the words for what was in my mind but I was always aware of a sense of waiting, waiting, waiting to achieve my degree, waiting to get away from my family and get out into the world, waiting, above all, for the turmoil of observations, impressions, half-formed beliefs and disbeliefs in my mind to take on some sort of coherence, to come out of chaos into order. I was waiting to find myself and to discover the nature of my rabbits.

In 1930, I achieved my degree but I did not get away from my family, for what became known as the Great Trade Depression had settled over the land and nobody wanted to employ a Master of Arts with good secretarial qualifications. Nobody wanted to employ anybody, so I went home to John, Uncle George, my aunt, my grandparents and The Colony. I would have been happy at The Colony but for the unspoken discontent in the air that a Master of Arts, whose education had cost a considerable amount of money, was milking cows, making butter and doing housework but I think now, that if I had stayed there, the pen would never have reached the paper.

I happened to read at this time the best-selling American novel *Flaming Youth* by Warner Fabian. The book was presented to me by a friend and I still have it so the quotation that follows is exact but it would have been exact even if I had not been able to check it. The printed word only corroborates what is engraved on my memory.

I do not claim that *Flaming Youth* is a great work of literature but I am grateful to it for this sentence that was written of one of the female characters: 'The layers of fat were insulating that soft and comfort-enslaved soul.' This was the first intimation to come to me that happy dreaming contentment can smother and choke the potentiality of a personality, can drug to death the desire to achieve.

In his foreword to the book, Warner Fabian wrote something else which I remembered. 'Women writers, when they write of women, evade and conceal and palliate.' *Flaming Youth* and its foreword were written in 1923 and I find it interesting that, in

1957 when, before acceptance for publication, *My Friend Muriel* was being reported upon by professional readers, my agent wrote: 'Both readers have commented on the narrator's self-portrait as unsympathetic.' In 1957 as well as in 1923, it appears, a little evasion, concealment and palliation would have been preferred on the part of a woman writer. The 'anti-hero' was now in being but it was not yet quite acceptable even to adumbrate the 'anti' in a heroine.

It was not until the early 1930s that my pen reached paper and from then forward pens, ink and paper became a constant problem. I worked at what I privately called 'neither flesh, fowl or good red herring' jobs, as a sort of secretary-companion-general-dog's-body to various women, lived-in and had a salary of twenty-five shillings a week. On this, I was expected to buy clothes for all occasions and clothes suitable for stays in places like Italy, Switzerland and the South of France. When I write of these foreign parts, it may sound as if my life were very interesting indeed but things are not always as they sound and seem. I think it summarises the way of life if I tell you that one employer and I, on our travels by car, chanced to arrive in Salzburg to spend a night during the period of the music festival. We spent the evening in a cinema, watching a film that we had both seen already in London, called *Fire over England* (starring Errol Flynn), with English sound and German sub-titles.

It was with this employer that I really learned about boredom. I myself was never bored – one could try to match the German sub-titles to the English sound, for instance – but I saw how my wealthy employer suffered from boredom. The layers of fat had insulated soul, heart and mind to the degree where she could take no interest in anything but moved from moment to moment in effortless passivity, as if the boredom acted like a drug. She always had to have something to 'do', like sitting through *Fire over England* but never did anything that called for the slightest effort or even understanding.

Repression and frustration have their uses. It is impossible to be bored if you are struggling all the time against odds and my odds were a dearth of paper, ink and the time to use them. I made most of my own clothes, made over to fit me cast-offs that my employers gave me, economised in every way, bought the cheapest seats at concerts and theatres and bought them at all only when the mental and spiritual wasteland threatened

17

to overwhelm me. From the best seats in theatres, I saw all the farces and musical comedies of the time. But economise as I would, there was never enough money to buy paper to write on or books to read. I wrote on opened-out paper bags, brown paper and opened-out envelopes and on Fridays, when I received my twenty-five shillings for the week, I would spend half-a-crown on white quarto and have a debauch during the nights of Friday, Saturday and Sunday. The writing was all done, of course, in secret or during the night for my various employers would not have approved of this absurd activity in 'their' time.

I had no friends in the real sense of the word because I belonged neither in the drawing-room nor in the servants' hall. I had a string of what are called boy-friends, some of them met in the drawing-rooms, some of them 'picked up' in concert halls or theatres but I was not deeply interested in any of them and as soon as one of them showed signs of moving towards a more intimate relationship, I took flight. They were merely an escape from the drawing-rooms and the current employer.

Yet, although I found my way of life unsatisfactory in the main, I did not try to escape from it for I could not think of anywhere to go. In spite of the boy-friends, I was still shy, reticent, with a very low opinion of myself. I was rather ashamed that I did not seem to want what other young women wanted, such as beautiful clothes, a 'good time', marriage, travel or wealth but I admitted this only to myself. Outwardly, I tried to conform but, inwardly, I truly was neither flesh, fowl nor good red herring, for this is what a writer is, a rogue who is outside any and every group, even the 'group' of writers.

In September of 1939, the Second World War broke out and when I look back to that date, I am as certain as it is possible to be that there is no pure good in human life and no pure evil. What led to that war and that war itself were some of the greatest evils in human history but for me that war was a release from bondage, from the bondage of a stagnant society bogged down in its own selfishness and self-satisfaction and from the bondage of my own self-doubts.

I found my freedom as a six-digit number, an aircraftwoman in the Women's Auxiliary Air Force, inside a high wire-mesh fence, behind the guarded gates of a Coastal Command station. My shyness, my reticence dissolved like mist in a barrack room shared with twenty-nine other women. I was no longer in the fashionable drawing-room in homemade clothes. I wore a uniform that was identical with the other twenty-nine uniforms but, at five feet nine inches tall and with shoulders broader than my twenty-two inch waist, I wore the uniform better than the other twenty-nine. On my first visit to the barrack square, I became the 'marker' of the two-hundred-strong squad and that evening, in the barrack room, when I elected to lie on my cot and read a book instead of going to the NAAFI with the other twenty-nine, they told me with cheerful frankness that I was a 'queer one' but they implied that they accepted me as I was. I hasten to add that the word 'queer' did not have, in 1939, the connotation that it now has in some circles. It was the first time that I had ever felt that I was accepted as myself and not as part of my family or an insignificant member of a student group or an even more insignificant companion-secretary and in being accepted as myself, the person who for convenience had been given a six-digit number, I accepted myself for the first time and began to feel that I had some particular, individual personal value. My astonished rabbits were still at the back of my mind but in that noisy rabbit-warren of a barrack room, it was impossible to write of rabbits or of anything else but when I became corporal in charge of the other twenty-nine, which happened within a few weeks, I thought of my airwomen secretly as my rabbits. I watched them, listened to them, helped them write their letters home, bullied them to bed when they came in drunk, forced them to wash and mend their underwear, man-handled them apart when they indulged in hair-tearing clawing quarrels and discovered some nine months later, when I was posted to be commissioned as an officer, that I loved them. I left them with my rabbit-warren of a mind stored with the things they had said and done and my heart full of love and admiration for their lusty courageous humanity.

Unlike Daudet's rabbits, my rabbits of the barrack room were not astonished when I told them that I was being posted for commissioning and would be leaving them. They were sad, one or two shed tears and in the end the oldest of them, a woman of nearly forty, summed up their thoughts when she sighed and said: 'Well, we're not surprised.' In other words, to be more grammatically correct than their spokeswoman, they were not astonished, but in my time with them, *they* had astonished *me*.

I had never known so much raw, rumbustious uninhibited life, I had made the discovery that I loved it and I was also approaching the discovery that you cannot write about rabbits, people, the Highlands of Scotland or anything else with any true understanding unless you love to write and love, also, the subject you write about.

In the eight years between 1931 and 1939, I had disliked most of my employers because they had presented me with little to like but after my nine months in the barrack room, I looked back with pity rather than with dislike. I now knew what it was to be liked and even loved, not as a child of my family but as a person in my own right and liking and loving beget liking and loving. When I was commissioned and posted to my new unit, which was a fantastic amalgam of nationalities, Army, Navy, Air Force and personalities that ranged from Freddie Ashton (now Sir Frederick Ashton) to a man who had spent his pre-war working life watching the movements of herring shoals in the North Sea, I found I could make friends.

The sole reason that I could imagine for my posting to this unit was that, in my time at Glasgow University, to obtain an arts degree, one had to take one science to degree standard. Being as unscientific as it is possible to be, it was fortunate for me that Geography was classed as a science and so, because I could read a map, I suppose, I was posted into Photographic Intelligence. All my colleagues in the unit were, in my opinion, much more intelligent and gifted than I was, most of them were better educated – there were professors of archaeology, botany and other subjects among them – but the barrack room had assured me that I too 'had something' and I found my place in this amalgam. It was made up of a very interesting group of rabbits indeed. I remember coming off a twelve-hour night watch and walking to the Nissen hut mess for breakfast with Pilot Officer Freddie Ashton. The orderly presented each of us with a plate of dehydrated re-constituted eggs which had been 'scrambled'. In the centre of each plate there was a little island of greenish-yellow vomit, washed on all sides by a little ocean of pale green liquid.

'Jane,' said Freddie, 'let's be seditious.'

'Yes,' I said, 'let's.'

When the above two lines of dialogue were read by my editor, he wrote to ask me what form the sedition of Freddie and myself took. My first reaction to this question was one of horror and dismay. Having known me for all these years, how could he possibly think me capable of sedition? When the first shock was over, I was interested to discover that my attitude to the words 'seditious' and 'sedition' was precisely what it had been thirty-four years ago when they were two of the dirtiest words in the language. That Freddie and I should contemplate sedition in 1941 because of some nauseating food was so unthinkable as to be extremely comical and I find it interesting that the contemplated sedition is no longer comical but extremely thinkable. My editor's department has given me an even deeper sense of having lived through much change than I had hitherto.

Most of my colleagues in this unit in its early days had been directly commissioned, had not come up from the ranks as I had and had never 'bashed' a barrack square. The Air Ministry, in its wisdom, decided that this unit must be 'licked into shape' and sent down a Warrant Officer (Drill) to conduct the operation.

We broke his heart and within three weeks had him on the run back to where he came from. The first crack in that hard heart was made on the first morning by a charming mediaeval archaeologist who had described his peace-time occupation on his official form as 'scraper of church walls'. He was a tall handsome man and was chosen by the Warrant Officer to act as Adjutant of the parade and was instructed in the commands that were to call us all to order. He was to call the male squad to attention first and then 'fall in' us women auxiliaries behind it but the 'adjutant' was a well-brought-up gentleman who believed in 'ladies first'. Having listened to the shouted instructions very solemnly, he strolled towards us of the distaff side, swept his hat off and said: 'Good morning, ladies. Would you mind—?'

As we walked back to our desks after this first drill, a Section Officer, one of the most individual members of the unit, said to me: 'Really, the impertinence of that young non-commissioned officer, trying to chase us all about as if we were – were – *rabbits*!'

I said in the letter that opens this script that the war years were sterile for me and by this I meant that to record the happenings of those years would be a sterile undertaking for me. It simply would not work. I have no gift for reportage. Life at the Photographic Intelligence Unit was interesting and very amusing but the Air Force had given me all it had to give me before I left the Other Ranks' barrack room. It had given me a spark of confidence, a fleeting spark that came and went, that one day I would be a writer.

Chapter 3

Why did you write seven novels before trying to get publication?
I did not think that any of them were fit for publication.

This script is doubling back on itself and going forward again as if it were imitating memory itself, so now we come back to my arrival in England from the West Indies in January of 1959 and I now quote part of a report which appeared in the London *Evening Standard* on the fifth of March of that year:

'A modest Scotswoman of forty-nine, Miss Jane Duncan sent the manuscript of a novel to Macmillan the publishers from the tiny village in Ross-shire where she lives. (Do not blame the journalist for inaccuracy. They work at great speed.) She had never before submitted anything for publication. The publishers accepted the book and asked for more. Miss Duncan sent two more novels and then arrived in person with four more. All seven books were written in the last two years. (What the journalist should have said was that the novels had been put on paper during the last two years but he was not to know of my reading of Daudet's rabbits at the age of twelve.) All have been accepted. The first is due to come out in May.'

From the early 1930s onwards, my life was punctuated by a series of bonfires and dumpings of closely-written paper of all colours, shapes and sizes. Each time I moved from one job to another, I had to get rid of my accumulation of paper or buy a large trunk to transport it and I could not afford to buy a trunk of any size. In the early part of 1957, I knew that, before very long, I was going to have to face the biggest and worst crisis of my life so far. I knew that my husband was going to die. One did not admit to this knowledge, one went on hoping and doing the best one could in each day that followed each day and a large part of each of my days was given to worrying about finance. The constant attendance of doctors and trained nurses

23

did not come cheap in a country where there was no free health service. When I jabbed that darning needle into the page of the *Writers' and Artists' Year Book*, therefore, it was a desperate throw. Before I burned the heap of manuscript that was taking up too much space in the linen cupboard, I had to find out if some of it might pay a doctor's bill. I was given at last the courage of despair, at forty-seven years old, to come out of the secret cavern that was my writing world and face the real world, let it judge whether or not I was a writer.

On the day that I sent *My Friend Muriel* to my agent, I wrote him a letter informing him that it would soon be followed by *My Friend Monica*, because *My Friend Muriel* was not designed to stand alone, but was a single chapter, as it were, in a planned series of some length. I wrote to this effect because at some time, somewhere, I had read that publishers were wary of 'one-book authors' but I think now that I scared the poor man witless and made him extremely wary of the kind of author I seemed to him to be. However, unaware of this at the time, I shipped *My Friend Monica* as soon as I had put it into typescript and, of course, following the encouragement of the acceptance of *My Friend Muriel*, I sent off *My Friend Rose* and *My Friends the Miss Boyds*. I then gave all my time, while I was making the decision to come back to Britain, to setting up the other three novels in my possession in typescript.

I arrived in London on the sixth of January, 1959, having arranged to send my crates of heavy baggage from Liverpool to Jemimaville, parted at the station from the lady named Muriel and her blue notebook and went to the hotel where my editor had booked a room for me. There were flowers in the room with a card from him and a message to the effect that he would call on me that evening.

I suppose most of us preconceive images of people we know of and are to meet for the first time and many letters had been exchanged between this man and me. He wrote with such kindness and understanding and also with so much knowledge of his publishing world that he made me, so ignorant of that world, feel that he must be a great deal older than myself and as I was nearly forty-nine at this time, I envisaged a man in his sixties at least. He would be short, bald and rather portly, I thought, with a round, kindly, wise face and would wear those spectacles that were crescent-shaped so that he could either look through them or over the top of them. I was extremely disconcerted, therefore, to encounter a man in his mid-thirties, with thick black curling hair, who was six feet four inches tall, very thin and seemed to be, although I thought I must be mistaken in this, even more shy and nervous than I was.

I was not mistaken, I discovered later, for he too had made a preconception based, I think, on the brash Janet of *My Friend Muriel*. At all events, much later, he confessed to me that he had expected a short, red-haired, pink-cheeked bouncy Scotswoman and was disconcerted by a tall skinny woman who was not even obviously Scots.

When he asked me if I would have a drink, like a fool I asked for whisky. I was so nervous that I forgot that I had eaten hardly any lunch at Liverpool, had been unable to eat any dinner and it was now after nine o'clock in the evening. Then, to make matters worse, a lady and gentleman arrived who were introduced to me as Mr and Mrs Maurice Macmillan. I became more nervous than ever and found myself drinking even more whisky. It is not surprising that I remember very little more of my entry into the writing world.

I do remember, however, my arrival at the offices of Macmillan & Co. Ltd. at about eleven the next morning. I paid off the taxi, the commissionaire opened the door, I crossed the threshold and became rooted to the spot with sheer terror. Macmillan, to the regret of myself and many other people, have now moved to more modern offices in another part of the city but the grandeur of the hall of those old offices is engraved on my memory for ever. It was oak-panelled, with many oak shelves full of books and on top of the shelves there were portraits of writers, not people like me but real writers like Rudyard Kipling and Edith Sitwell and out of this hall rose an impressive oak staircase which branched off at a landing in two directions. On the landing, there was a stained-glass window and on its broad sill sat the daddy of them all, a life-size bust of Shakespeare, in the full colour of scarlet doublet and all-seeing dark eyes, holding in his hand a long white quill pen.

Weak at the knees, I followed the receptionist past him and up again into a wide upper hall and from the oak panels of this the oil-painted faces of past Macmillans and their colleagues gazed solemnly down upon me, more in sorrow than in anger, it seemed, at my presumption in entering their portals, so that

I wished my too solid flesh would melt into the Persian carpet without leaving the slightest mark.

In the editor's office, though, things were less terrifying, for he was – and is – a mischievous and humorous man and his office, which he had decorated with stuffed birds under tall Victorian glass domes, seemed to poke fun at the Victorian grandeur beyond his door.

I am sure that many people could have entered this building without being impressed to the point of being overpowered as I was, but character is very much the product of race, heredity, environment and the *mores* of one's immediate family. I am a Scottish Highlander and all my ancestors as far as they can be traced, which is to the Jacobite Rebellion of 1745 on my father's side, have been Highland. The Scottish respect for learning used to be world-known and this respect was even more marked in the Highlands than in other parts of Scotland. The Highlands did not produce many writers before the present century but it has to be remembered that the population was sparse and ill-educated. My grandparents, I think, would be the first of my forebears to be literate. But on second thought, that is not accurate. My Great-great-uncle Kenneth was literate. He was the uncle of my grandmother but he was virtually of her generation, being only about ten years her senior. They were literate enough to write their names and a short simple letter, literate enough to calculate the incomings and outgoings of a small croft, literate enough to read the reportage in the local newspaper but this elementary literacy made their respect for more advanced learning all the greater. My mother and father read for pleasure the novels of Walter Scott and Charles Dickens and although my mother died when I was ten, she lived for long enough to imbue me with something of her own deep respect for books and the people who wrote them. Scott and Dickens were gods in the eyes of my parents, creatures endowed with gifts far beyond the reach of common men, creatures who inhabited a remote mysterious world which soon became, in my imagination, a sort of cloud-capped Olympus.

One has to remember, too, on a more material plane, that in the early decades of this century, there was an aura of the 'upper class' about writers, a belief that to be a writer, you had to have 'private means'. People like my parents did not know that Dickens was a child of the slums but they did know that

Walter Scott was *Sir* Walter Scott and that Byron was *Lord* Byron. (Incidentally, Lord Byron was an Aberdonian and therefore a Lowlander.) And my parents did not aspire to read Shakespeare and did not know that he was the son of a glover.

Now that we are on the edge of the last quarter of this century, a century that has brought so much social change, it is difficult to keep in mind the depth with which the idea of class penetrated into people's minds. Only the other day, I listened with amazement to a cricketer on television talking of his game during the 1930s. 'We professionals,' he said, 'travelled third class and went to the Duck and Pheasant when we got out of the train. The amateurs travelled first class and went to the five-star hotel up the road.' He was speaking of men who were members of the same cricket team and I found my mind boggling until I gave it a shake, sent it back to the 1930s and remembered that I used to read of cricket matches played by the 'gentlemen' against the 'players' and that such a division was accepted without question. Is it any wonder, therefore, that people like my parents and grandparents regarded writing and the arts in general as the prerogative of the 'upper classes with private means'?

Naturally, their attitude had rubbed off on to me for they were all people of strong character who were sure that they knew how to bring up their children and how to direct them in the way they should think and go and but for the accident of Alphonse Daudet and his rabbits, I doubt if I would ever have questioned any of their tenets. Even *with* the rabbits of Provence and The Colony giving me their strong backing, I felt presumptuous in these oak-panelled Persian-carpeted halls and I wished I had retained my rabbits as the illicit secret they had been for thirty-eight years.

My nervousness abated, however, when my editor took me to another office which contained perhaps some ten men and women, among them Mr Maurice Macmillan of the night before, the production manager and the art editor. I was more interested than nervous now for I had never before realised what a complicated process is the production of a book, how perilous the journey between my ill-typed script to the finished volume in its gaily-coloured dust-jacket. I was interested but wading in waters deep and unknown, a fact of which all these people seemed to be totally unaware.

27

The production manager led me aside, showed me the spine of a dummy book with *My Friends the Miss Boyds* printed on it and said: 'I think you should have some sort of colophon.' For all my life-long reading of the dictionary and other books I could not remember ever having come across the word 'colophon'. 'A what?' I said, my mind boggling around colitis and the intestines in general.

'What about a thistle, in gilt, of course, like the title?'

'A thistle? Oh God, no!' I said.

The man looked hurt, as well he might, for he could not know that although I am a Highlander and proud of it, I have a horror of those aggressive tartan-waving Scots, so common overseas, to whom my brother and I were wont to refer as 'the wha's like us brigade'. He sighed sadly, laid the dummy book aside and said longingly: 'Kipling had a swastika.' It was only now that I understood what he meant by colophon and I was sorry about his hurt feelings and his air of frustrated longing but who was I to set myself up beside Kipling? Then, in the same second, I had another thought which I spoke aloud: 'And Somerset Maugham has that queer Moorish sign!' The man brightened and agreed that this was so. 'What about a little fir tree?' I asked, hoping to make him happy again and that is how, in answer to those who have asked, my Reachfar series of novels came to have a little fir tree on their spines.

The other incident of that morning that I remember vividly was the art editor producing the jacket that had been designed for *My Friend Muriel*. The design covered the front and the spine, the back was blank and the publicity manager suggested that the back of the jacket should carry some material about the other three books I had sent them. At this moment, Mr Maurice Macmillan said to me politely: 'And do you intend to go on writing?' and I replied: 'Actually, I have three more novels in my luggage at Liverpool.' He asked me what the titles were and I said: '*My Friend Annie, My Friend Sandy* and *My Friend Martha's Aunt*.' Mr Macmillan handed the jacket to the art editor and said: 'That makes seven you've got. You ought to be able to do something with that.'

When I had written my ill-natured letter to the editor, saying that his reference to my tiny paw made me feel like a monkey on a stick, he had replied with his customary courtesy and good nature, thanking me for my 'act of faith' in allowing *My Friends the Miss Boyds* to be published first. I do not know if any writer other than myself has had three novels accepted sight unseen but this struck me as a quite extraordinary act of faith.

Having made the acquaintance of my publishers, I travelled home to Jemimaville, of which I hope to tell in a later chapter, then returned to London, arriving on the morning of the third of March. I had been sent a programme of proposed activities for the next four days, mostly meetings with librarians and the managers of bookshops. There was an appointment too for the taking of a photograph, for I had not been photographed since the days of the war. All went to schedule until the evening of Thursday, fifth of March, when the *Evening Standard* went on the streets with the report I have quoted. I suppose that there had been no murder, political scandal or royal engagement that week for, on the Friday morning, the stately home of Macmillan was like a fortress besieged by reporters, a huge – considering the cause – press conference was held at a hotel in the afternoon and the entire riot culminated in the B.B.C. studios at Lime Grove, where I appeared on a programme called 'Tonight'.

What I am trying to stress in this saga is the freakish absurdity of my position. Had the Fates combed the world, they could not have found anyone less well-equipped than I was to cope with what had happened to me. My secret vice of writing was now blinding me with its public glare; people were asking me how and why I had started to write in the first place and I did not know the answers. I was physically and mentally exhausted with the events of the day and now, towards six in the evening, my editor and I – buoyed up with whisky at this stage – were in this chauffeur-driven limousine going to a place called Lime Grove where, presumably, more people were going to ask me more questions about this writing thing that I knew nothing about. Why couldn't these Lime Grove people have come to the hotel to ask their questions like all the others? Who did they think they were anyway? But I did not say any of this to my editor for I was still trying to do, politely if possible, all that these act-of-faith publishing people asked of me.

The chauffeur stopped the car at a wide, canopied entrance, handed me out and the editor and I went into a reception hall. I thought it was another hotel and another conference. Then, a very pleasant, fashionably-dressed young woman led us through a heavy door, rather like the door of a vault, into a passage that was full of these heavy doors and on into a small cocktail lounge. Here, a pleasant-looking man with spectacles met us and said: 'I am Cliff Michelmore,' and I had a curious impression that he expected me to know him and when he asked whether I would like a drink or would I prefer coffee, I asked for coffee in a tone that I hoped would indicate that of *course* he and I had known each other for years.

You will recognise that I was in a television studio but you must also recognise that the Fates had chosen the one person, probably, in Britain that evening who had never seen Cliff Michelmore and whose total experience of television was to have heard the news read at her brother's home once or twice several years before.

I know that it must seem strange that even I was so stupid but people who know a thing with much familiarity do not think it needs any explanation to anyone. My friends at Macmillan had mentioned the word 'tonight' several times and had seemed to be very pleased about it but that did not surprise me for I also was looking forward to the night and the end of all these questions people were asking.

Then, before I had time to drink my coffee, Cliff Michelmore handed me over to a young man with very long, thick eyelashes who led me through one of the heavy metal doors into a little alcove which held two chairs and a small table. He seated me on one side of this and himself on the other and further along there was another alcove which held two young men with guitars. It was like a pleasant sort of nightmare. Only the alcoves were lit and lit very brightly, while outside of us there was a huge dark cavern where big mechanical shapes, vaguely like agricultural tractors, moved to and fro silently and eerily. Then a young woman pounced out of the darkness and with a huge puff dusted my face and the face of the young man with heavy, dark yellow powder, just as the guitars began to play. I liked the music so I leaned out of our alcove and peered along at their's the better to see the young men and was suddenly recalled by the voice of my own young man saying rather loudly: '*Tell* me, Miss Duncan—' and we were back among the questions again. I do not remember what he asked me or what I answered but I am certain that he must have thought that I was less than half-witted. All I remember is the yellow powder falling like Scotch mist from those long eye-lashes of his as he spoke. And, for sheer idiocy, I had not yet done my worst. The young man, thankfully I am sure, led me out into the passage where the young woman who had welcomed us on arrival caught me by the shoulders and almost hugged me. 'Miss Duncan, you were marvellous!' she said. 'Not a bit nervous, *so* relaxed and this is "Tonight"!' I thought she was out of her mind or thought that I was out of mine and to correct such an impression, I said: 'I know. I didn't think it was yesterday or tomorrow,' whereupon my editor led me rather hurriedly back to the limousine.

There is a little tail-piece to my first television appearance which is, I think, of deeper interest than the appearance itself. My brother, at this time, was a schoolmaster in a country district of Aberdeenshire and the publicity manager had telegraphed him to watch the 'Tonight' programme. (Even when I was asked for my brother's address, I did not understand what was happening, so dazed was I.) John, my sister-in-law, my little niece Shona and her brothers watched this family curiosity but as soon as it was over the telephone rang. The caller was a farmer's wife who had never seen me and she said: 'Mr Cameron, did you watch "Tonight"? Was that lady novelist a relation of yours by any chance? She's awful like wee Shona.' I do not think that anyone, seeing my niece and me standing side by side, would see much resemblance between us but by some trick of the camera the resemblance came through to that woman. Our parents gave my brother and me our lasting respect for books but it seems that they also gave us physical characteristics that are equally indelible.

Later that night, my patient editor put me on the train for Inverness and with gratitude I shut myself into the privacy of my sleeper cubicle but the attendant came to ask if I wanted tea in the morning. When I opened the door, he looked at me, poked his pencil into my chest and said: 'Here, *you* were on *television*!' By this time, I knew that I had been on television and did not want to be reminded of it. I wished to be alone with the terrible thought that there had been all this brouhaha about seven novels, the first of which would not be published until the seventh of May. Two months was an interval long enough for the tide of good fortune to turn against me and my tiny paws began to sweat coldly that night in the train and went on sweating until *My Friends the Miss Boyds* came out on schedule.

The tide of fortune came the way of my publishers and myself or was it more a question of our combined faith than mere fortune? However it was, *My Friends the Miss Boyds* turned into something of a best-seller but this was less important to me than the knowledge that I had, after all, written a book that was fit for publication, was published and was being read, apparently, with pleasure.

And now some people began to ask me: 'How does it feel to be famous?' I did not feel famous and had never in my life wanted to be famous. You may remember that I said earlier that when I was a university student, I regarded Milton as an old bore who could not even 'think straight'. I feel less harsh about Milton now but in my opinion he had one thought that was not straight, the thought that he voiced in *Lycidas*:

> *Fame is the spur that the clear spirit doth raise*
> *(That last infirmity of Noble mind)*
> *To scorn delight and live laborious dayes—*

I regard the desire for fame as the product of an *un*-clear spirit, the infirmity of an ignoble mind. A writer who writes to achieve fame is writing for the wrong reason and is therefore a dishonest and in my opinion a bad writer. The only honest reason for writing is the desire to write, to share, to communicate, something one has to do whether or not it brings any reward.

Chapter 4

Why do you live in a remote place like Jemimaville?
Jemimaville is my place.

I think that most writers have places on the face of the earth, places that possess them. I would go so far as to say that, if Russia had been a tiny country like Luxemburg, the Russian novel would have been a completely different genre, for in every Russian novel, for me, Russia herself is always the dominating character with the exception, perhaps, of *Anna Karenina.* I come away from every Russian novel with a mind filled with the vast steppes, the birch forests, the winter cold and the summer heat and I think it is their love for their land that gives the Russian writers the ability to describe it so well, that it is indeed this love for their mighty land that lends such mighty power to their pens.

I have been described as a 'regional' writer, a term which reviewers use in a derogatory sense as a rule, but I have never been able to understand what 'regional' as applied to a writer means. Sometimes it seems to mean a writer who writes of any place outside London. If this is the case, there are a tremendous number of regional writers, from Shakespeare down the centuries to Thomas Hardy. Shakespeare's regions were the courts and battles of history and the woods of Henley-in-Arden, although sometimes he called these last Bohemia, Illyria or A Wood near Athens. Hardy's region was Wessex and his novels are all the better for it. Can you imagine them without it?

After my first visit to my publishers in January 1959, I took the night train to Inverness where I was to be met by my Uncle George and his friend Hugh, the owner of the local garage. When the train puffed about five hours late into Inverness station backwards, as the old steam trains always did, any warm sense of homecoming that I might have had was totally dispersed, for it was freezing cold, the platform covered in frozen snow and large flakes of snow were still falling. By the time my luggage had been piled into the car and we were driving towards the outskirts of the town, my blood, after ten years in the tropics, seemed to be frozen in my veins and my teeth could not chatter because the joints of my jaws were rigid.

'Stop!' I said through clenched teeth to Hugh. 'Stop at that pub before I die of cold,' and in the pub I said to him and my uncle: 'Whisky?'

Hugh moved away from us and my uncle dug me in the ribs and whispered: 'Hugh never touches drink now since the police caught him!'

'Won't you have anything at all, Hugh?' I asked.

'Och, well,' said Hugh, as if indulging me in a whim, 'I'll take a double gin and lime, if you please.'

I suddenly knew I was home, home in the place where there is no 'drink' except whisky. A little later on, I was lunching at a hotel with a local woman to whom I said: 'A drink?' 'No thank you,' she replied. 'I never drink. I'll just have a brandy and Babycham.'

I am writing, however, of fifteen years ago. Nowadays, the distinctions about drink are less nice.

The journey from Inverness, the non-drink double gin having been taken, was appalling, with the car having to be dug out of a snowdrift on the way and the arrival at the cottage was worse. Inside, it was colder than out-of-doors for my uncle and Hugh had left early in the morning, only to hang around Inverness waiting for my late train. The fire was dead in the grate, the wind whistled in under the doors and round the window-frames as I sat shivering while my uncle piled on paper, wood and coal and got a fire going. A bath, I thought, a hot bath and then like a drench of icy water over me came the memory that this cottage had no bath, no water supply, that every drop had to be carried from the village pump. I am mad, I told myself now, stark staring raving mad! How could I ever have imagined that I could live here after a bungalow in the tropics and half-a-dozen servants? After that big room in my friend's house where I had been waited on hand and foot?

The fire began to blaze, I began to thaw out and followed my uncle when he went through to the scullery. Here, there was an electric cooker and on it a large pot of broth ready to be heated. We had no water but we did have electricity, but the house had no electrical appliances except the cooker and one ceiling light in each room. This was the house to which my father had retired at the end of his service in the police and it had been the joy of my stepmother's heart, but she was one of those housewives, common in the Scotland of her time, who regarded a house as a possession and showpiece, to be kept scrupulously clean and tended, not as a home for people to live in. The place, therefore, was crammed to the ceilings of all seven small rooms with possessions – furniture, ornaments – but there were no electric fires or bedside lamps.

When The Colony was sold, my uncle had come to the cottage to stay with my father and stepmother, for the brothers had a lifelong devotion to one another and after my father died in 1951, my uncle remained at the cottage, much as he disliked old Kirsty, as he and I called my stepmother. He stayed to keep in order the beautiful garden that my father had made and to 'keep an eye on' the house which my father had left to my brother and me but of which Kirsty had lifetime use. However, in the summer of 1958, Kirsty had gone away to live with a sister and since then George had been in the house alone. He had done his best to keep it clean, which was nearly impossible, so cluttered was it with furniture and there was little cheer or comfort about Kirsty's buff wallpaper (that it did not show the dirt was the housewifely virtue that she saw in this colour) and shiny buff linoleum on the floor while the slate grey of the 'parlour' wallpaper and carpet was even more grim.

It was over three years since I had last seen my uncle, there had been much sadness in my life since then of which neither of us wanted to speak and my mind was burdened by this extraordinary thing I had done in writing a book, wondering how I was going to explain myself to my uncle. So far, nobody close to me knew of my book except the friend who had housed me in Jamaica and my brother and his wife.

As the broth heated on the cooker, I said, in order to say something: 'When did the police catch Hugh for drinking and driving?'

'About a year ago. They threatened to take away his driving licence.' The indignation in his voice gave way to the dry chuckle that I had heard so often in childhood, in the barn or the granary or everywhere that was out of my grandmother's hearing. 'Do you mind on yon time just after the war when you were at The Colony on holiday and Hugh drove your father and them all in their tall hats to old Sandy's funeral?'

We were off. Time crumbled and disintegrated and we were back in The Colony stable. 'And when they all came out of the pub afterwards,' I said, 'Hugh took the Humpy Bridge over the Red Burn too fast and all their top hats were squashed as flat as pancakes!' In uncontrollable mirth, we held on to the scullery table and were only recalled to sense when the broth boiled over.

This little story of Hugh who 'never touched the drink now' is my token of gratitude, long after his death, to a man I liked very much and who, by being the character he was to talk about, helped me through a very cold difficult return to my own place.

After we had drunk the broth, I took a deep breath and said: 'George, I have written a book.'

'A book?'

It was late into the night and the fire had burned a lot of coal before this extraordinary thing was accepted and digested.

'They paid me a hundred pounds for it,' I said, 'and maybe it will make a little more and maybe it won't. Maybe none of the other six will make anything either but if they don't maybe I can get a job of some kind.'

'We'll manage,' said George, who despised the title of uncle. 'I have the pension and I still have a pound or two at the bottom of the kist.' [This last will be explained in due course.] 'You keep going at the books.'

He rose to his feet and his seventy-nine-year-old back was as straight, his shoulders as square as they had been in his photograph as a Seaforth Highlander at the turn of the century, but he was not as tall as then. His spine had shrunk. 'You boil up the kettle,' he said. 'I'll go up for the two bottles I put in your bed and we'll fill them again. I made your bed in the west room. I am in the east one.'

The west bedroom was dank and cold with years of disuse and seemed to be made colder by Kirsty's economically dim bulb in its blue porcelain shade in the middle of the ceiling but I unpacked hurriedly what I needed and got into bed. I had been sitting against the pillows with two cardigans round my shoulders and a hot-water bottle on either side of me for a long time before I discovered that some of what I had instinctively needed to unpack had been some sheets of paper and my pen. I, who had not written a new word in the ideal haven in the tropic paradise, now, in the freezing cold of an attic bedroom in

Jemimaville had begun a new novel. Its title was *My Friend Flora* and it is set in this part of Ross-shire which is my place.

It is proverbial that birds of a feather flock together but I tend to avoid the company of other writers with the exception of the very few who, when we do meet, never talk about writing. There was a time when I thought that writers and artists of all kinds were made of a clay much superior to my own which may account for the terror that George Orwell inspired in me, but that day is long past. Most writers are of a very ordinary clay indeed although I have met one or two very notable exceptions.

And I would rather live in any jungle than in the 'writers' world' of any city, with its pub that is noted for its writing clientele. Writing is essentially a solitary occupation and I think it probable that many a book is talked out of shape or even out of existence over beer in some bar. Nor can I think of any atmosphere more arid than that of a 'literary' party. Indeed, it is worse than arid, it is an acid atmosphere which seems to bring out the worst that is in writers, and writers, being moderately articulate as well as moderately literate in the main have a lot of worst that they are able to express. One can see the women putting a price on the other women's clothes and see the thought behind the calculating eyes: 'I wonder how many thousands she has sold *this* time?' and one can see the men jockeying for position next to whom they think is the big shot who may be able to do them the most good. But perhaps, on second thought, this sort of behaviour is not peculiar to the world of writers. I suppose that any party of people drawn together basically for financial reasons is doomed in this way. One young man, though, who was peculiar to the writers' world was the one who gloomed through a dinner party, drank too much and at last said to me in a self-pitying voice: 'I have just torn up a *whole novel*, a good novel but they wouldn't take it. A year's work, a whole *novel*, just torn up!' I knew I ought to tell him for his own good that I had torn up or burned at least fifty but it would have sounded like one-upmanship (which is something I have never liked). I did not tell him either that I had torn them up or burned them because they were not novels but only miserable bundles of paper and that probably what he had torn up was only a miserable bundle of paper too.

One writer I met only once and that towards the end of his

long life, unfortunately, and who truly impressed me was Neil Gunn. I remember now the joy with which I read his *Morning Tide* when it came out in the early 1930s. As I contend that all writers have or should have a 'place', Neil Gunn was a writer of place and that place was the Highlands, as mine is, but it was not this kinship or even the quality of his writing that caused my admiration. I spent a long evening in his company, hardly speaking unless he asked me a question, but I watched him and listened to him and was overawed by his sheer quality as a man. I was overawed by his serene calm, his modesty, his humility and his air of spirituality. He took me back to those days of innocence when I believed that writers must be people of great mental stature, for this is what he was, a man of great mental stature who could wear serenity like a garment and now and then afford a sparkling jewel of kindly mirth to light the depths of wisdom in his eyes.

In the course of this evening, there was a little incident that delighted him. By this time, I had moved out of the cottage into the converted barn where I now live and had lent the cottage for a few days to my friends, the Harts. Professor Hart, at that time, was Professor of English Literature at the University of Virginia and a long-time admirer of Neil Gunn. The Hart family consists of Rus, his wife Lorena, their son Russell and their twin daughters, Ruth and Priscilla who, at that time, were about eleven years old.

Discovering that, although we lived only about twenty miles apart, I had never met Neil Gunn, Lorena decided to give a little dinner party, made up of her family, Neil Gunn, Ian Grimble and myself and to set the scene a little further, I should explain that the cottage is surrounded by trimmed privet hedges.

Like myself when I returned from the West Indies, the Harts thought that all Highland men drank whisky and when they spoke of a drink to Neil Gunn, he floored them by saying: 'I'll have some gin, please.' I have discovered that many whisky drinkers take to gin when they grow older.

Lorena looked nonplussed and embarrassed and I made to send her son Russell the few yards down to my barn for some gin but, before I could speak, the little girls said in unison: 'We'll bring you some gin, Mom,' went out for a second and returned with a bottle three-quarters full of gin.

'Where did you get that?' their father asked, his eyes popping.

'In our garden hedge. There's some more in the back-garden hedge,' they assured Neil Gunn in case three-quarters of a bottle would not be enough.

I spoke now to Neil Gunn for the first time without being asked a question. My kind neighbour who trimmed the hedges for me, I explained, did not 'drink' while working but always kept an odd bottle of gin or two in the hedges, in the apple trees and in his hen-house in case he became thirsty. Neil Gunn laughed, a deep silent sort of laugh, a loving laugh at a story peculiar to a Highland village of the kind he loved. When I assured him that he would be welcome to a tot of gin out of the hedge bottle, he remarked that neighbourly gin always tasted better.

Not only do I live in Jemimaville because it and its environs are my home place, I like to live here because I am regarded as one of the natives, the neighbours, a member of a family which has lived in this district for a long time. The embarrassing fact that I make my living by writing is never mentioned by these Highland people who are polite to the point of being hypocritical. If a Highlander, myself included, is going to cut your throat, he will set about it with a smooth air of politeness. It is only if he likes and trusts you that he will take the liberty of being rude to you. My writing, in the eyes of the neighbours, is like a disability with which I have been born, like a club foot or a hare lip, which it is impolite even to notice, although I feel they may say to one another in private: 'What a queer thing to have happened in the Cameron family! And her mother's folk were decent hardworking people as well!'

My neighbours do not entirely trust me. I feel that they glance at me in their minds as an older generation used to glance with their eyes at my grandmother who was believed to be something of a witch. But this sidelong glance at writing and writers is not peculiar to this village. There is a general distrust of writers on the part of people who do not write, a distrust that is difficult to define. It is as if the writer is suspected of having a built-in secret weapon against which other people must be constantly on their guard.

And my neighbours distrust me because I do not 'work'. They know that I am not descended from the gentry, that I have no inherited wealth but I contrive in some mysterious – and therefore quite likely dishonest – way to provide myself with food and a roof over my head. As one of George's old cronies, now dead, once said: 'You can't call sitting on your backside all day with a pen in your hand *work*!'

Allan Campbell Maclean, a writer who lives in Inverness, tells the story of giving a lecture to some local group. The chairman who was to introduce Allan asked, as is usual in these affairs, for a few personal details of the writer for his introductory speech. Allan gave him a few facts about the course of his life and the books he had written, whereupon the chairman said: 'I see. Now, tell me, what do you do for a living?' But writing is a form of work and you can earn a living from it if you are lucky but I think that, like most forms of work, you have to enjoy doing it before you can do it well. I do not subscribe to all this talk about 'the agony and hell of writing'. If there is agony and hell, it is self-sought.

I think that, as well as benefiting from a geographical 'place', writers benefit from a sense of place in the literature of their country. I have said how, as students, my colleagues and I thought that the-powers-that-were of our Faculty were very fuddy-duddy in their emphasis on the classics of our language. Now that I am three times and more the age that I was then, my view is different. I now see literature as a flowing river which has its source in some long-dead human mind which was the first to develop and exercise the desire to communicate. All people who are honestly trying to write are trying to contribute to this river, to be borne along with it into the future, but only very few succeed. Many sink without trace because their contributions are not of the true element of which the river is made. Many are washed on to the banks or caught in the roots of riverside growths such as contemporary fashion or politics, or beached on the shallows of a too-personal idiosyncrasy. But those classics which we students affected to despise are the true element of the river. If they were not, they would not have survived.

As students, we were all for the new. We did not know that there is nothing new under the sun and did not understand that, as surely as we were born out of our fuddy-duddy parents, the new is born out of the old, the future is born out of the past and must, in the very nature of things, have in it something of that past.

I believe, therefore, that the writer begins by being a reader who absorbs into his being the essential element of the river

40

that flows down from the past and then tries to add his own contribution in a form that is relevant to his own time. It is accepted psychologically that the child who feels insecure finds life difficult and can make life difficult for those around him, while the child who has a firm sense of belonging is more likely to grow into a socially acceptable being. In a similar way, it seems to me that the writer who has some knowledge of his literary ancestry has a better chance of being accepted into the main stream. It is always an advantage to know the place you came from and the place you are at now, in order to know where you are going next.

I am not a literary critic and would never denigrate the work of any honest writer – the denigrators of the past have so often been proved wrong – but I am worried by a sort of rootlessness in much modern writing, a feeling that it has come from nowhere and is going nowhere, never going to find a *place*. I know that such places fall to very few but I think the drive behind the humblest writer, if he is honest, must be the desire to achieve that permanent place.

There is one more aspect of the writer's 'place' that I should like to mention. When I wrote above: '– to add his own contribution in a form that is relevant to his own time,' I originally wrote: '*her* own contribution ... *her* own time,' but altered the pronouns to the more traditional form to avoid sounding too aggressively feminist. My belief is that what I should have written is: '*its* own contribution ... *its* own time,' for I think the true writer is, in mind, a dichotomous creature, half-male, half-female, built on the Chinese principle of Yin and Yang. A thing that should please the Women's Liberation Movement, however, is that sex has no effect on place or rewards in the writer's world. Here, the book is the thing and it makes no difference whether its creator is a man or a woman. This is why we of the female sex dislike the word 'authoress' which, according to my dictionary came into the language in 1478, when women were either beasts of burden or playthings. In our world where we have our place, we are neither authors nor authoresses, we are quite simply writers.

So I am a writer who lives in Jemimaville but do not stress the writing too much when talking to my neighbours.

Chapter 5

Is your Uncle George the George of the Reachfar novels?
Yes, but my uncle was a great deal more.

It has been said often enough and perhaps too often that only God can make a tree and I am certain that only God can make a man, especially a man like George.

When I used to be sent home to The Colony with a label bearing my name and address pinned inside my coat, he used to meet me at Inverness and from that moment I became his shadow for the rest of the holidays. We would cross the station platform and board the little Black Isle train that would take us to Fortrose where the horse and trap were stabled and as soon as we were seated he would say something like this: 'We might take a notion and go down to Wick. Tell me, now, were you ever down at Wick?' I, a bookish child, as I have indicated, would at once think of the map of Scotland and visualise the position of Wick much nearer to the top of the map than Inverness where we were now sitting, then laugh at him and say: 'You *are* stupid, George! Wick is *up*, not down!' whereupon he would look amazed and say: 'Mercy me, do you tell me that now?'

He was the only adult at whom I was allowed to laugh and call stupid for even my stern grandmother did not try to make me pay even lip-service respect to this 'clown' as she frequently called him.

George had a subtle way of turning the world upside down to give a new view of it and to me as a child, being 'well brought up' which meant being restricted in many ways, he gave a freedom with his sudden suggestion: 'We might take a notion and go down to Wick.' We were not going to do it, of course. We were in the train for Fortrose and would drive the trap to The Colony as the rest of the family required of us, but he had indicated that we were free to take a notion and go down to Wick if we really wanted to. And behind his words, somehow, there was implied a gleeful mischief at the consternation of the family if we really did take a notion and go down to Wick.

George kept the flag of freedom flying for me at a time when the child tended to be the prisoner of the adult world. Children-should-be-seen-and-not-heard, speak-when-they-are-spoken-to, Mother-knows-best, don't-dare-to-speak-back-to-your-elders-and-betters and many more were dogmas that were seriously believed in. Parents sincerely believed that these restrictions were good for the child and perhaps, indeed, they were but George did not believe in restrictions of any kind. He did not see the need for them or for the law itself because he never, I think, felt the evil desire to hurt or harm anyone or anything, and his concern to help and protect, especially the vulnerable or young, was very strong. It was very seldom that George took part in an argument or made a strong statement of any kind, but when he did it was the statement to end all statements on that subject.

I was a quiet, solitary, dreamy adolescent, the very type to be an annoyance to my irritable, voluble, opinionated stepmother. I was and still am utterly uncompetitive in every way, would not play games like other girls, did not like parties and did not care if Elsie was the prettiest girl in the school or Mary the star of the hockey field. I was just plain unnatural, Kirsty said, and perhaps she was right.

Well, in the final days of my final year at my academy, I did one of my unnatural things. I won the Dux Medal of the school and forgot all about it until my father looked up from the little local newspaper and said: 'Listen to this – "The Dux Medal of Lenzie Academy has been won by Elizabeth Jane Cameron, Police Station, Croy." ' He put the paper down on his knees and asked: 'Is this true?'

'Yes,' I said. 'I get it on Prize Day.'

'And you never told us?' Kirsty shrilled in her high Aberdeenshire voice. 'Well, of all the unnatural ways to carry on—'

For most of the time, Kirsty called me a fool when my father was not present and I am sure that in spite of the medal she still thought I was a fool, but the medal could be used as a pawn in a one-upmanship among the neighbours.

'Why didn't you tell us?' my father asked quietly.

'Sorry, Dad. I just forgot.'

Being non-competitive, the medal meant nothing to me. What was important to me at that time was that a week or so later, it would be the holidays and The Colony, and that after the holidays I would go to the university. The medal, for me, was

43

the merest incident and eminently forgettable but although my father was still looking puzzled, I could not find the words to explain. Passions are difficult to explain, even when one is quite experienced in life and moderately articulate and at seventeen my passions were The Colony and learning about literature, but I did not recognise them as passions. They were great secret things that were part of me and for which I had no words.

Until I left for The Colony, Kirsty seemed to speak – Kirsty always sharply and shrilly 'spoke', she never softly talked or eruditely conversed – continuously, day and night, of nothing but the medal and my unnaturalness, and on the first evening that she and my father joined us at The Colony about six weeks later, she told the story of my unnatural forgetfulness with many repetitions to the entire family and then fixed her dark, beady eyes on me and said: 'She *forgot*. How in the world did you *forget*?' She had brought the medal in its black velvet case with her and now produced it to dangle it before my eyes. 'Look at it, solid gold and she *forgot*! Why would anybody in their senses forget a thing like this?'

'I'll tell you why,' said George suddenly, his voice sounding very deep and quiet after Kirsty's shrilling. 'She has enough sense to have better things to think about than that bloody silly bauble.' The medal was returned to its case, shoved into a drawer of the dresser and was never mentioned or seen again until George and my father found it when they were preparing to sell The Colony about twenty-five years later.

George always seemed to know the 'why' of me and of people in general without words of explanation and this understanding came, I think, from his complete selflessness of interest. He was so interested in the other person that he knew that the phrase 'down to Wick' would, for the type of child I was, open the way for me to 'correct' him and he knew that to correct an adult was the deepest pleasure for a child of my time and background. And he could go from being my age to being his own much older age in the twinkling of an eye, exactly when it suited him. If I played a trick on him, he made it much more enjoyable for me by saying: 'What a terrible thing to do to your poor old uncle!'

My first clear memory of him is when I was four years old and he and I got into serious trouble. At this time, I had a baby sister, Catherine, who was to die in infancy of appendicitis. She had been born in April and in the summer of that year she, my mother and I were at The Colony and Catherine spent most of her time sleeping in the old wooden cradle in the back bedroom. I know that I have said that I was an only child until the age of ten when my brother was born but Catherine's was one of those short little lives that left hardly a mark on anyone except her parents.

George and I had this ferret called Angus who lived in a box in the barn. Most females of all ages are terrified of ferrets, and even I myself would not care to handle one now, but at that time Angus was an extension of George and much loved by me. We had strict instructions from my grandmother that the ferret was to be used only to keep down the vermin and that he was to be worked only when we had netted the site of operations all round so that he could not escape. Early on this summer morning, however, when we went to give some oats to the horses before harnessing them, a big rat jumped out of the oats-chest and disappeared down the stable drain.

'The dirty boogger!' said George, then stood looking down at me for a moment before saying: 'Just take a run along to the house and see that Herself is busy at something.'

'Oh George *Cameron*!' I said, for I knew he was thinking of employing Angus, but I did as he told me and came back to report that my grandmother had started to bake.

We smuggled Angus from barn to stable under George's coat and put him down the drain. First we waited, then we poked in the drain with sticks, then we went out to see if Angus had emerged in the midden but no Angus appeared and in the end we had to admit to one another that we had done the unforgivable and had let the ferret go off on the loose.

'Ferrets are very thrawn beasts,' said George, worried. 'As like as not he'll come out of some hole at Herself's very feet, the devil.'

But all day passed without Angus appearing and as we all gathered for supper, my mother went through to the back bedroom to see that Catherine was all right. There came a horrible scream which sent my grandmother and my aunt running through, then there came a chorus of screams.

'Was I not telling you about their thrawn-ness?' George whispered to me.

I ran into the bedroom. My mother was clutching Catherine,

45

my grandmother and aunt were clutching my mother and the baby and all their eyes were fixed in horror on Angus, who was sleeping, curled up in a cosy little white ball, at the foot of the cradle. I picked him up. 'I let him out of his box,' I said. 'I didn't mean to. He just got out.'

Before my grandmother could get out of her fright and into her tirade, George appeared and looked down at me very sternly. 'How often have I told you to leave that bloody ferret be?' he asked. 'Take him back to his bloody box this minute you damned interfering little b—'

'George Cameron!' said my grandmother. 'Hold your wicked tongue this minute! What language is that to be using to the bairn? How was *she* to know that that dirty brute might come up anywhere about the place? Take him back yourself and lock him in his box and don't set foot back in this house until you learn to watch your words!'

Like the medal, the ferret was not mentioned again.

That was in the year 1914 and George was thirty-five then, with his seven years' service as a Seaforth Highlander in Egypt and India long behind him but he could reach with me, as a child of four, such an understanding as would outwit even a very cunning old woman like my grandmother. He made me understand without direct words that she would not scold *me* too severely for letting the ferret escape, let me take the blame and then deflected her wrath on to himself. In his own words, spoken later: 'If she had known it was *me* that put him down the stable drain, her tongue would have clapped on like a kirk bell for a week.' I think that this was the first time that we combined to stop my grandmother's tongue from clapping on like a kirk bell but it was not the last.

George was a man of peace. When war broke out in August of that year, he made no secret of the fact that, although he had army training, he did not want to re-enlist and his character was well enough known, not to say feared, for no hysterical patriot to offer him a white feather. He did not make a fuss, he merely said that he was not going and it was quietly and wisely decided by the powers-that-were that he should be retained on the land.

His Army escapade was typical. It was the time when he really did take a notion and go down to Wick. He really did, as I have told in one of my novels, go to Inverness to a circus, joined the Army on impulse and did not come home for seven years. But it was the peace-time Army, the showpiece prestige Army of the British Raj and George was one of its showpieces. The smartest soldier on parade each morning got 'the stick' for the day, a little swagger cane that released him from all duty except as messenger to the Officers' Mess. 'I got the stick most days,' he told me once. 'It was worth a bit of extra pipeclay to get it. Nothing to do all day but drink beer on the verandas with the officers' wives when you took their letters to them. I've never in my life seen such a bunch of useless besoms – they wouldn't even nurse their own bairns – as these memsahibs but they were very kindly in the way of beer.' This interests me as an oblique comment on the British Raj.

George enjoyed his years in the Army in spite of wearing seven pleated yards of heavy tartan kilt in the heat of Egypt and India. I have never met anybody who did not like George, he would have been popular in his regiment and certainly the friends he made wrote to him and came to stay at The Colony until, one by one, they died. But there was one thing he did not like. 'I could never do with the way some of the whites treated the natives,' and there was one sight which remained a horror haunting his mind. The swill from the barrack messes in Egypt was put into barrels and each day an Arab with a mule cart came to collect the barrels. Outside the barrack gates there was a great mass of hungry people holding bowls and the Arab, who had a ladle, sold the swill to them for 'a piastre a dip'. 'Just like this stuff we are giving to the old sow here,' George would tell me as we tipped the kitchen refuse bucket into the trough. 'To treat people yon way just can't be right.'

In 1915, George married but his wife died a year later at the birth of their first baby and the baby died too and those people, like my baby sister Catherine, were never mentioned again because George did not want them mentioned. George gave out happiness but kept his sorrows to himself.

Naturally, my most vivid memories of these early times are of the occasions when he and I were in trouble, which was fairly frequently. We used to be sent with the horse and trap to Cromarty each Friday to exchange farm produce for groceries and while I went to the fishertown to listen to the lore of Bella Beagle or one of my other friends, George would go to the pub to meet his cronies. It was Bella Beagle who proved to me that haddocks swam in the Sea of Galilee by showing me the marks of Christ's forefinger and thumb just behind their gills and it was she who told me that the robin got his red breast by picking the thorns out of Christ's brow, so that his blood dyed the feathers of the breast. Bella Beagle – her real name was Gunn, but all Gunns were called after the family boat *The Beagle* – was a very interesting talker, so interesting that one Friday I stayed with her too long and George had difficulty in finding me in the crowded warren of the fishertown. We were in danger of being late home for supper and thus incurring the wrath of my grandmother but George did not make a fuss. He understood, as no other adult of my acquaintance did, that when you were hearing interesting things, it was easy to forget things like supper and even the wrath of Herself. He did not scold sinners, he helped them out and all he said now was: 'We'll take the short cut over the face of the hill.'

I was startled. 'With the *trap*?' The short cut was a rough, stony track used only by pedestrians. I did not understand then, as I have come to understand since, that I was my grandmother's safeguard that 'that clown' would not stay at the pub all evening and forget to come home. I do not mean to suggest that George was a drunkard. I never in my life saw him drunk but people loved his company and would keep urging him to stay.

Usually, on these visits to Cromarty, I was the timekeeper. I would leave my fishertown friends, go to the pub stable, yoke the horse and bring it round to the door of the bar for George, giving him the excuse: 'It is time for me to take the bairn home.' On this evening when I had failed in my duty and then asked the startled question about the trap, he said: 'Herself will never be a bit the wiser.' This, of course, made the hazardous journey attractive, for it was always enjoyable to get the upper hand of Herself, even if your triumph had to be kept secret.

So we set off across the face of the hill, the mare picking her way carefully among the boulders, the left wheel of the trap high, the right wheel low on the sloping road.

'Take the reins for a bittie,' George said, 'while I fill my pipe.' Another mark of George's difference from other adults was that he never implied that there was anything one could not do.

'No, you can't churn the butter,' my grandmother would say. 'Wait till you are older.'

'*You* bake scones?' Kirsty would say. 'Get out of my road.'

George was different. 'Can I help to carry the corn up to the granary, George?'

'Surely. I'll be glad of a hand,' he would reply. 'Turn your back and I'll load you,' and I would set off up the steep granary steps, holding the top corners of the sack over my shoulders, convinced that I was carrying a hundredweight of grain, and even when I discovered that George was supporting the weight of the sack, I did not mind. He always convinced me that, without my help, corn would never reach granary, sheaves would never be stacked, fields of turnips never be hoed, but on this day when he gave me the reins, he overestimated me. (Here is another newly-discovered truth about him. He always overestimated the worth of people, never underestimated it.)

I could drive the trap or a box cart on the road, I could even keep the plough pair on a straight furrow, for all the horses were trained by George and knew their work but while he was filling his pipe, it seemed to me that Dulcie was heading too far towards the downward side of the track and I reined her back to the middle. The mare had more sense than I had. In changing her direction I had brought the high wheel of the trap on to the line of a large boulder, the wheel rose upon it and our whole equipage tipped over, including Dulcie, while George and I went rolling down the hill in a welter of packages of groceries.

In silence, we picked ourselves up, unyoked the mare who rose unhurt to her feet and I gathered up the groceries and dusted them off while George righted the trap and re-yoked Dulcie. I watched him walk round the trap and dust some earth from the spokes of the downward wheel, so ashamed of my incompetence that I could not speak.

'It is a mercy it was not *down* to Cromarty we were going, with the eggs and butter and honey and all, for that would have been a right clarty mess,' he said, 'and I'll thank you just to watch your tongue when we get home.'

'Watching my tongue' meant that I was to leave the explaining to him should any questions be asked about the dent in the wartime tin of corned beef.

'It was a mercy that it was not *down*—' George could always

49

find the mercies in life, all the things to be thankful for.

And now we come again to my first morning at home in the cottage in 1959, the morning after I had begun the new novel. I had scrambled some eggs for breakfast and when George had eaten his share, he said: 'That was good. I can make porridge and broth and semolina pudding but I can do nothing with eggs but boil them.' Then that mischievous look came into his eyes as it had done when he put Angus down the stable drain. 'In bed last night,' he said, 'I had an idea. If things don't go right and we get hard up, we can pawn your medal.'

My mind, naturally enough, went to the 1939–1945 war. I had won no medals. 'What medal?'

'*Kirsty's* Dux Medal, her that can hardly write her name!'

'I did some thinking in bed last night too,' I said. 'We have plenty of rubbish to get rid of without bothering about the medal. We are going to sell most of the furniture that's cluttering up this house. You go along to the shop and get about fifty tie-on labels and then tie one on every useless stick and every stick you don't like and I'll write to the auction rooms and tell them to come and collect.'

We had a riotous time. We sold most of the furniture, had a telephone installed, had plumbers make a bathroom in the box-room upstairs, install a sink in the scullery and connect us to the water main that had recently come through the village. Then we had electricians rewire the house and bought a variety of electrical appliances.

'We have spent a lot more than we got for old Kirsty's furniture,' I said when the plumbers' bill came in.

'And we'll spend a bittie more for luck,' said George. 'There is a bonnie wee pan along in the shop that will be just the thing for that chocolate pudding you make.'

He had a very sweet tooth and was addicted to chocolate pudding but I have always thought that the 'bonnie wee pan' was the final act of faith that made *My Friends the Miss Boyds* the success it was.

Our neighbours, at this time, did not know about my writing but the unexpected television appearance burst upon them as it had done upon me. George was the only man in the district, I think, who did not see it for we did not have a set and did not have one until many years later.

At that time, there were several men of George's age in the

village but they were all old and invalid in some way while he was still young and fit. I discovered that, rather than sit with Kirsty in the evenings, he had been in the habit of accepting their invitations to come and watch horse racing, show-jumping and such programmes and I encouraged him to continue in this way, not for his own sake but for that of his hosts. The show-jumping invitations were merely an excuse on the part of lonely housebound men to get George's company for an evening but no Highlander likes to be beholden to anybody, so as long as we had no television set in our own house, the excuse held water and George was having show-jumping in exchange for his company. Unlike my father, his brother George was no reader of fiction and as I wrote those words I made another discovery about him. Many readers have asked me if there was a tradition of writing in my family and I have always replied in the negative but now that I re-think, the dedication page of *My Friend Muriel* reads: 'For the oldest of my friends, that great teller of stories, George—' My editor assures me that my most valuable asset as a writer is my ability to tell a story so I have this minute discovered that like the Aberdeenshire farmer's wife seeing something in me of my niece Shona, there is something of George in me. If he endowed me with something of his own ability to tell stories, I am more grateful to him than ever.

So he was a teller of stories, not a reader of them and his reading was normally confined to the newspaper but he read *My Friends the Miss Boyds* and his reaction was: 'These two, George and Tom in this book, are right comical fellows.'

Everyone who has met George and has read the books tells me that it has captured something of his quality, but George, with his total unawareness of self, saw two other individuals, comical fellows. George was the very reverse of the person who says to writers: 'If I told you about my life you could write a book about it.' It never occurred to George to look at himself and find himself interesting. He was too busy looking at other people.

In our village, at that time, there lived an elderly holier-than-thou woman who spoke to me over the garden gate about *My Friends the Miss Boyds* more in sorrow than in anger. There was a lot of very coarse language in it, she said and some things that were really not one bit nice. When I came into the house,

George said: 'What was she on about? She looked as if she was preaching a sermon.'

'She was.' I told him what had been said and ended: '– and she thought the scene in the old quarry was not one bit nice.'

'*She* shouldn't be talking,' said George. 'With *her*, though, it wasn't in the old quarry. It was down in the Little Birches.'

Journalists and radio interviewers called at the house, people of a kind that George had never encountered before but at seventy-nine years old he took them all in his stride and indeed many of them became more interested in him than in me whom they had made the journey to interview. His most extraordinary friendship of all was with my editor who came for a weekend as soon as our bathroom had been installed; the most unlikely friendship, one would think, between a young man from the sophisticated world of London publishing and an old man who was a Highland crofter to the backbone.

George appointed himself as the guardian of my privacy. The burst of publicity and the moderate success of the book caused the holiday-makers of the summer of 1959 to seek me out. I am sure the visits were well-intentioned but if I had entertained all the visitors, I would have had little time left for anything else. Also, I have an idiosyncrasy which may or may not be common to all writers. The unexpected, a sudden interruption of any kind can 'throw me' for as long as a week. The flow of writing can be blocked for days by a three-minute telephone call from some stranger. George seemed to have an instinctive understanding of this as he had of so many other things and he became very proficient at turning visitors away without hurting their feelings.

Knowing by this instinct that I could cope with any interruption if given warning, at breakfast on the thirty-first of October, he said: 'This is Hallowe'en. The guisers will be out in force this evening.' The ancient custom of 'guising', of the children dressing up and painting their faces out of recognition and calling to entertain their neighbours on Hallowe'en is still practised in this part of the country. At this time, I had finished the first draft of *My Friend Flora* and had embarked in a rush of blood to the head on *My Friend Madame Zora* which I regard as my contribution to the genre of the detective story.

'I am going along to the shop to get five bob's worth of

pennies and some nuts for the guisers and we have the apples from the garden,' said George. 'Mind you, if they can't sing or dance or something, I don't let them in. Some of them are no better than beggars, just out for all they can get. Do you think I am right?' George was not one of those people who are convinced of their own righteousness in all things.

'Quite right!' I agreed with him. 'The idea is that they should entertain and be rewarded.'

So a number of parties of guisers were given pennies and turned away from the door but I shall always remember a party of eight; four little boys and four little girls as they were recognised by George in the end who said at the door: 'We are guisers and we want to sing for you, George.'

'Come away in then,' he said.

They formed into a semi-circle round the fireplace and began to sing in their clear tuneful child voices a melody that I recognised. It was that of a hymn of the extraordinary Society of Shakers of the eighteenth century which, in Jamaica, had been sung by members of a modern religious sect to new words. The children had probably learned their version at school and they had more new words to the charming old melody:

> *Dance, dance, wherever you may be*
> *For I am the Lord of the Dance, said he—*

And the children formed into a ring, incorporating George but not myself into it, as they danced and sang the final verse, so that one of my many mind pictures of George is as Lord of the Dance.

Thus, my Uncle George was the George of the Reachfar novels and a great deal more. Tom of the same novels is another facet of him and Angus the Shepherd in my novels about the Cameron family for young people is yet another. The real George was a man so complex and of such stature that one can put down on paper only little bits of him. Fictional characters are usually made up like those Identikit pictures that the police use, the eyes from the description of one witness, the hair from that of another. For a fictional character, one usually takes a trick of speech from one person, a trick of gesture from another, adds a little something of one's own and welds the lot together. But my Uncle George was and still is, in memory, such a deep

53

quarry, so rich, that it needs only a little bit of him to make a fictional man. To portray the whole real man is away far beyond my powers.

Chapter 6

You have travelled quite a lot. Is travel important to a writer?
It may be for some writers but I don't think it is for me.

Earlier, I stated my belief that 'place' had importance for many
writers but I suppose that there is no statement of this kind to
which glaring exceptions cannot be found. Many writers, for
example, have taken against the places and countries of their
birth and have found other places, but these are still 'places'
in the sense of being environments where these writers feel at
home.

It may be that some writers find their 'environment' in constant movement from place to place and in this connection
Somerset Maugham springs to mind, the Somerset Maugham of
tropical islands and the China Seas. But as well as having a place,
a writer has a time and Somerset Maugham was born at a time
that was opportune for him to travel to, write about and
generally open up to his audience remote and exotic places that
had been only very sparsely written of before. It seems to me
that there would be little point in travelling to Tahiti at the present day in search of material. Tahiti is no longer remote or
exotic. But, in any case, I distrust the 'search for material' approach. I think that the best material is generated from within,
out of an observation of people and events that is largely subconscious. I certainly could not say: 'I am going to write about
a murder in Honolulu,' visit Honolulu for background material
and proceed to write a novel. This is not how things work for me.

All my characters arise out of real people I have met and in
some cases not even met but merely seen across a hotel lounge,
for instance, and sometimes only a few words or a gesture are
necessary to sow the seed of a fictional character. *My Friend
Rose* grew out of a brassy-haired drunken woman I once saw in
the 1930s in the club-house of an exclusive Home Counties golf
club and she became part of the story of *Janet Sandison*. She
was typical of her generation and the time, that original brassy-
haired drunken woman. *My Friend Cousin Emmie* grew out of

an old English spinster I met in a train from Glasgow to Inverness in about 1946, who opened a packet of sandwiches and said: 'I never eat railway food. You never know what might happen.' It was a simple matter to transfer her from the Glasgow-Inverness train to a transatlantic ship for her incorporation into the story of Janet.

But to find such people it is not necessary to go to the Home Counties or to travel from Glasgow to Inverness. I could probably have found both of them, or something very like them, within a few miles of my home, for the characters I am interested in and interested in creating are the typical, the ordinary, the ones you meet anywhere and every day. These people are the most interesting for, when you study them, you have to come to the conclusion that there is no such person as the typical, the ordinary, that you meet everywhere and every day. You can find old spinsters in trains or in large villas but they are all different from one another and there is no need to go to Tahiti to find the exotic and strange. You merely have to take a good look at the people all around you.

I have never been to Tahiti but I have been further afield to the brave new worlds depicted in science fiction and films in the scientific genre, and what do I find, what do you find? People, ordinary people, some of them as odd in appearance in their plastic trappings as the child guisers of Hallowe'en were odd in appearance in the dress-up clothes and mother's make-up but they have still the foibles and failings of ordinary people and are moved by love and hate, the issues of life and death. Even when he tries to write of distant planets, man cannot get away from his own 'ordinariness' that is yet individual and extraordinary. It seems to me that no matter how far one may travel or how widely one lets the imagination range, one cannot get away from the human condition and at the same time one will never catalogue its multifarious manifestations.

This is my view and it is entirely opposed to that of Somerset Maugham who was a much more successful writer than I am and who left at his death funds for the Somerset Maugham Awards for young writers, the awards being conditional on their being used for foreign travel.

I am very doubtful about this stipulation but then I am doubtful about all awards, grants and 'helpings-out' of young writers. I think a little struggle and even frustration and repression may be good for the young. The ungenerous will say: 'Just because you had it hard, you want the young generation to have it hard,' but, truly, this is not my attitude.

In my early life, I was often unhappy it is true, but I was not aware then of having it harder than anyone else and I would not, now, change one jot or tittle of my experience even if I could. No. It is that I believe that writing, like murder, will out and the better executed murders are probably those that come out later rather than sooner. To obtain power from steam, one does not let it dissipate itself, one compresses it to danger point and then canalises it.

Of course, among writers as among those who try to practice any of the arts, there are the exceptions. I know as well as you do that Keats died at twenty-six and Shelley at thirty, both leaving a body of good work behind them but as a general rule the master-work by youth is extremely rare. And Keats and Shelley were poets, romantic poets and youth is the time for romance and poetry. I wrote what George would have called 'a fairish puckle' of poetry when I was young which contributed to my various bonfires, but the world can rest assured it has suffered no great loss. I was never a Keats or a Shelley.

This brings me, however, to another aspect of travel. In a lifetime, one does not travel through space only but through time as well, an obvious truth which tends sometimes to be forgotten. A writer belongs to his time in the first place and to eternity only much later, in the unlikely event of his survival at all. Our present age is unlikely to throw up a romantic poet for it would be difficult to write an 'Ode to a Skylark' in an age when the poor bird has to struggle for a scrap of a sky that is dense with jet aircraft.

In *My Friends the Hungry Generation*, I put into the words of the babe and suckling, Liz, some words that are worth thinking about. She is being rebuked as unchristian for her attitude to her school playground enemy and she replies: ' "Love thine enemies," Christ said, but I don't think there could have been people like Amanda Shand in *His* time.' We of the human race are at enormous pains to make the world and our lives in it more complex from age to age and the writer tries first to understand his own complex experience and then tries to communicate that understanding to anyone who cares to read him. To do this it is not necessary for a writer to travel to Peking or Kalamazoo. A journey round the insides of his own head and heart will do very well.

This does not mean that I am denigrating the travel book which is so popular with armchair travellers. Any travelling that I have done has been fortuitous. In my earlier life it was forced on me by the exigencies of earning my living and later because my husband took a post in the West Indies. Two years ago, I went to the United States to visit friends but I would never board an aeroplane simply to visit a *place*. Again, I am not denigrating travel undertaken for its own sake but stating a personal attitude. I do not believe in the constant truth of the cliché that travel broadens the mind. The joke about Blackpool fish and chips being in demand by British visitors to the Costa Brava illustrates my belief that a mind that wishes to remain narrow will remain narrow no matter how far the body that contains it may travel, and a mind that wishes to broaden itself can do so in Jemimaville.

I could not go to Paris for a weekend and write a novel set in Paris. I have spent several weekends in Paris but have never written about that city. To write a novel set in a certain place, I have to live in that place for a number of years and my life has been made up of twenty-one years based in Scotland, seventeen based in England, ten based in the West Indies and another sixteen based in Scotland and as a consequence most of my writing has been based in Scotland.

As I tried to demonstrate in *My Friend Sandy* and my novels set in the West Indies, it is true that people react strangely when living within a culture that is not their own but for the reaction to come, they have to live within the culture, not merely travel through it, still clothed in their own culture to which they will shortly return.

This brings me back to my belief that the writer and perhaps everyone else is most true to himself in the place, the environment in which he feels at home. This is certainly true in my own case. I did not like life in the West Indies. Tropical islands are not all as pictured in the travel brochures. Jamaica, the island where I spent most time – my visits to other islands were very brief – is very beautiful in its tropical way although, by 1958, when I left it, much of it was falling victim to the concrete and neon of the tourist trade. But, for a Highland Scot, the heat and humidity were appalling and the mosquitoes and other

58

insects a constant irritation to the skin and a fret to the nerves. Many of the whites on our plantation claimed never to have been bitten at all but the fact was that they could be bitten without having any immediate reaction. I, however, in spite of screened windows and netted beds, was perpetually bedizened on face, arms and legs with great red lumps that had at their centres gleaming jewels of watery yellow pus. That the negroes and other whites, who were fond of saying I made a fuss about nothing, were bitten, although they did not show the scars as I did, is without doubt, for malaria was endemic among the negroes and I was the only white on the plantation who never suffered from it. Perhaps my red and yellow lumps of reaction were a blessing, although they did not feel like it at the time.

Our drinking water supply was the rain catchment from the roof of the house which was canalised into a large concrete tank in the garden. This was drained off once a year for cleaning, at which time a foot's depth of drowned lizards and other livestock would be shovelled out, smelling abominably, into a mule cart. Naturally, all this water had to be boiled for household use but for someone who thought of water in the terms of the crystal spring that bubbled up through the moor at The Colony, the water from the garden tank had no appeal. In the course of ten years, I must have drunk a fortune in imported soft drinks, for liquid in that heat was a prime essential. And beverages other than soft drinks were consumed in quantities too large to be beneficial. The tropical climate had a bleaching draining effect on the whites, sapping away all energy both mental and physical and it was easy to give way to the stimulus of alcohol which brings me, in this travelling chapter, to another point.

Many writers are alcoholics, many die of alcoholism or of ills to which alcohol has been contributory. I feel sure that the incidence of alcoholism among writers is higher than in any other one group and having at one time nearly become a victim myself through a combination, I suppose, of the writer's temperament, the tropical social life and my own frailty, I have given some thought as to why this should be so. It is extremely difficult to describe a certain state of mind that even a writer of only minor talent can reach. A pressure can build up in the mind, which can extend itself to a physical sensation in the body, of a force clamouring for release but no form of effort, mental or physical, can bring about this release.

Thomas Wolfe is, I think, one of the great writers that America has produced and in his *The Story of a Novel* he writes: 'At the end of the day of savage labour, my mind was still blazing with its effort, could by no opiate of reading, poetry, music, alcohol, or any other pleasure, be put at rest. I was unable to sleep, unable to subdue the tumult of these creature energies, and as a result of this condition for three years I prowled the streets—'

Wolfe was a man of enormous stature, both mental and physical and the greater the writer, the more 'savage' the labour, the greater the 'blaze' in the mind but to lesser people the savagery and the blaze are just as overpowering for, being lesser, they have less resources to pit against them. The phrase in the above quotation which interests me most, however, is: '– alcohol, or any other pleasure—'. I agree that no form of pleasure can act as an opiate for this writer's curse but alcohol, imbibed away beyond the point of pleasure, can stupefy even the greatest mind, as Wolfe himself discovered. A colossal man, he could become colossally drunk but I do not wish to give a false impression of him in this connection. He did not die directly of alcohol. He died of tuberculosis of the brain but I am sure that the alcohol did nothing to assist his body in fighting the tuberculosis in his bloodstream.

Incidentally, Wolfe was an incessant traveller throughout Europe and his own huge country of America, but all his novels are centred on simulacra of the little town where he was born and grew up, Asheville, in North Carolina. My grandmother said many things which I have proved to be true and one of them was: 'What you learn young you never forget.'

I 'put up with' Jamaica, complaining as little as I could, not only because I was happy with my husband, a Lowland Scot who was more adaptable to hot climates than I was. He had worked in many of the hot countries of the world. Everyone knows how usual it is to find Scottish engineers in ships and the same is true of factories on sugar plantations. I 'put up with' Jamaica also because it gave me what Britain could not – servants to do the cooking and housework while I tried to write. I feel no guilt about this. Our servants were well paid, fed and housed and treated more like human beings than I had been during the 1930s, although they did not travel to Salzburg at our expense to see Errol Flynn in *Fire Over England*.

Still, as I have described Janet Sandison superimposing the topography of Reachfar as a transparency over the map of St Jago, I superimposed my part of the Black Isle over the map of Jamaica, so that Montego Bay was Dingwall and Port Antonio was Cromarty. I was not homesick, I was merely holding fast to the place that was essential to me.

In the final analysis, I suppose, I place little value on travel because I am a woman of a race whose traditional abode was the glen of the clan. The men might go on a cattle-stealing expedition into the glen of the clan on the other side of the hill, but the women stayed at home. I know that here you can hardly wait to point out to me that there are Scots, especially Highland Scots and their descendants, scattered all over the face of the earth but in my turn I would point out to you that the Highlander becomes an expatriate mainly through economic pressures. They did not leave the Highlands to wander the earth looking for the strange and new. The David Livingstones were Lowlanders. The Highlanders left in the main because they were forced to go, in masses as at the time of the Clearances when the landlords decided that sheep were a better paying proposition than people, but long after the Clearances, the drift continued although less dramatically.

My grandmother had eight children, three boys and five girls. Of these, a boy and two girls died comparatively young but of the remaining three girls, one went to the United States and two to Canada, while my father left the Highlands for the Lowlands and George went to Egypt and India.

My father did not go south to join the Dunbartonshire police from choice for, at heart, he was always an exile and a displaced Highland crofter during the time he was in the south and when he retired on pension he came back here, bought the cottage out of his savings and worked on The Colony with George until it was no longer economical to work it at all.

George, an honest man, would have been the first to tell you that he did not join the Seaforth Highlanders to fight for his country or for Old Vic, as he called Queen Victoria with scant respect. He joined the Seaforth Highlanders when, at the circus, he chanced to meet a young Seaforth who was a native of Cromarty with whom George had gone to school and who told him of the ease of Army life compared with that of the ploughman and the Army rations that were so much better than the ploughman's porridge for breakfast, salt herring and potatoes for dinner and porridge for supper seven days a week. And George left the Army and came home because there came a day when, being the man he was, his conscience told him that his father was getting old and needed his help on The Colony.

Most people agree that there are few finer sights of a martial kind than a kilted Highland regiment on the march with a pipe band at its head but George and many of those who were with him in the regiment would tell you that for them Queen and Country didn't come into it. The Highland Regiments, in their heyday, were made up of mercenary soldiers who could find no other way of making a living.

I find now that trying to answer this question about travel and the writer has been, for me, a little voyage of discovery. I have discovered that I am no traveller, not even a traveller through life, for I tend to stand still and let life come to me. I have told you that although I rather despised the way I earned my living during the 1930s, I made no effort to better my lot but when the war came in 1939, the wealthy kind of women who employed women like me began to travel very fast in the direction of the safety of the United States. I had to get a living somehow and I took the simplest way out by joining one of the women's services. And once in the service, I was the most passive and obedient of members. I did not apply for commissioning. An officer did it on my behalf. I had never thought of such a thing for myself. I did not ask for postings to particular places or try to distinguish myself in any way. I merely did what I was told and went where I was sent. I was the most complete of fellow travellers, now that I think of it, but I did keep a watch on the other travellers, a thing I do by instinct, like breathing, a thing that I seem to have been doing all my life.

It has been said that it is better to travel hopefully than to arrive but I am not sure whether I agree. As a child, I used to travel with great hope on that Glasgow to Inverness train and more hopefully still in the trap from Fortrose to the march gate of The Colony and the arrival was always the great grand climax to the travelling, a joyful climax that never failed me. Coming from Fortrose, we came through the march gate at the south-west corner of the moor and travelled north-easterly over the track through the heather which was dotted with the pale mauve of wild orchis and scattered, in some places sparsely and in some places more densely, with fir trees, where the wood pigeons made that sleepy gurr-gurring sound. Then the long low white-washed house and steading would show between the trees, with my grandmother and grandfather out in front, warned of our approach by the sheep collies.

I know now that throughout all my physical travels, I wanted to make a final journey through the moor to that house and stay there. I have not achieved this. I have achieved only the next best thing, a converted barn down on the shore, two miles below at the bottom of The Colony hill. I am content to have, physically, the next best thing, for in my mind I have The Colony itself, the place known to you as 'Reachfar'.

Chapter 7

*In the Reachfar series, one of your characters says that we don't
live life, that life lives us. Do you believe this?*
*I think we are all the victims of our times and of the weather
of the world.*

By 'life living us' I mean that there are in life circumstances,
pressures and experiences which are forced upon us, that are not
matters of our own choice. We cannot choose the life-style into
which we are born, we have no armour against world cataclysm
such as war and we cannot control the effects these powerful
circumstances have upon us. On a lesser scale, we cannot choose
entirely the people with whom we come in contact and we cannot govern entirely the effects they may have upon us. It is with
this element of chance contact that I have been concerned in
much of what I have written, the creaking rusty hinge of what
one might as well call Fate, that fickle whimsical interference
that can work upon us without our knowing it.

And to add to the difficulties, personal contacts and world
events can be double-edged in their effect upon us. In a relationship between two people, the greater the love, the greater the
sorrow when the relationship ends, as all relationships in the
long run must end and a world event such as a war, while con-
taining much evil for many, has also a potential for good. In
my own case, as I have said, I recognised my own identity for
the first time as something of value under war conditions and I
regard this recognition as a small grain of good in a vast desert
of evil.

As I wrote in the letter to my editor which opens this book,
the war years were some of the most sterile of my life and there
was very little in them that I wish to record but it is only now,
when trying to answer more fully the question which heads this
chapter, that I have come to understand, I think, why the war
years meant so little to me. I did not live those six years. They
lived me.

We have the evidence of the pyramids, the works of Michelangelo, the music of Beethoven and many other things to prove that man is a constructive, creative animal and the creative instinct is the dominant one in any artist, however minor. Except for a few months, my war years were spent in the main Photographic Intelligence Unit. The earliest of those years were spent in gathering from aerial photographs information about every kind of enemy activity on the continent of Europe. Every shipyard, wireless station, railway yard, airfield, every installation of every kind was closely examined and recorded in minute detail with one end in view, their future total destruction. This work ran counter to my deepest instinct and instinctively, I think, I developed a resistance to it, a resistance of non-thought, a mental opting-out. I turned into a pair of keen-sighted eyes peering through a stereoscope at enemy-occupied territory and a hand holding a pen that recorded what the eyes saw.

When the war entered the phase of Allied attack, the protection afforded by non-thought became even more necessary, for we at the Unit were among the first to see on photographs the destruction of the Ruhr Valley by the floods of the broken Mohne and Eder dams, the ruins of Dresden and the liberated victims of Belsen, human beings reduced by beasts to bestiality.

When I was demobilised in the autumn of 1945, I went home to The Colony for a short holiday and among the trees of the moor I faced the fact that I, in my small way, had been as bestial as the beasts of Belsen. I had been caught by the weather of the world and had let myself 'obey orders', just as the guards of the concentration camps had done. It was a sickening wounding experience in self-discovery and there was no comfort in the excuse that the Nazi will to destroy all that stood in its path could be overcome only by the destruction of Nazism. The fact remained that I had behaved counter to my deepest and I think my best instincts.

At that time in 1945, I could have put none of this into words. It seems to me now that I was in a state of shock for my only conscious need was to get away from my family, from everybody I knew and do something, anything that would occupy my mind in a constructive way. The desire to write had left me. This was my invisible war wound and it took a long time to heal.

It was easy to escape from one's inner self in the grey dreariness of the postwar world, where so many petty restrictions made the business of living from day to day difficult. I took a post as

65

secretary in an engineering firm in a grim little Lowland town, a smug lace-curtained little place which is characterised in my memory by the story of two of its inhabitants. They were a man and wife who lived for twenty years at opposite ends of their grey stone, lace-curtained cottage, never seeing one another or speaking to one another until one day the man was seen, lying dead on the floor of his end of the house by an inquisitive neighbour who peered in through the window. In the local weekly newspaper the death was announced by his wife and followed by the words: 'Oh for the touch of a loving hand and the sound of a voice that is still.' This bleak mean sort of hypocrisy used to be a feature of many Scottish towns, both Highland and Lowland but I think that, at long last, it is dying out.

There was something furtive and suspicious in the very air of this town and it did not welcome strangers like me. The war had made it even more suspicious of strangers by placing on its outskirts a camp for Polish soldiers and although they had gone before I arrived, I learned what it felt like to be an unwanted foreigner.

When I first arrived, I went to live in the home of my employer and his wife and it took some weeks of searching before I found another lodging. This was behind some lace curtains which concealed a drunkard who maltreated his wife, who took in lodgers to keep a roof over her head and the lodgers were a sour, elderly spinster and myself who had a cold bedroom each and were expected to have our meals together, sharing a sitting-room with a meagre postwar coal fire. The elderly spinster and I met on terms of cold barren civility and no more, for she was a native of the town and as suspicious of 'incomers' as the other inhabitants. Very soon, I was going to my lodgings only to eat and sleep, for the only place in this town which held a welcome was my office and there was plenty to do there, so much, indeed, that there was no time to think of anything except which problem to tackle next.

My employer was a man who had been given few educational advantages but who was endowed with an inventive ingenuity in engineering that amounted to near-genius. He had invented a revolutionary heavy plough which he was going to put into production now that the war was over and to this end he had engaged me to 'run the inside', by which he meant manage the office. My first sight of this office was on a bleak, grey November morning in 1945. It was a rectangular room with two windows on one side and a third window at the end opposite the doorway. By this window, a man was standing, his profile towards me as he looked out at the leaden sky and I can remember my thought in that very first moment: 'He is very ill or very unhappy or both,' but the thought was at once overlaid in my mind by practical things and never recurred until many years later amid much sorrow.

'This is Alec,' my employer said and the man's expression changed as he came towards us. 'He has just come out of the Army. He's going to run the outside.'

Our employer, I was to discover, was interested in nothing but selling his product in order to obtain money to invent and produce further products. Only with some coaxing could I induce him to sit still for long enough to sign a few letters and his method of dictation to me was: 'Write and tell them to take a running jump to themselves' or 'Write and say the plough would do it standing on its head'. The office was a chaos of dusty mail, much of it unopened. There was no filing system, no system of any kind and the work force was being increased daily with no record being made even of the workers' names for the method used by 'Boss', as we called him, was: 'You're a welder? Right. Go and see Alec. That's him down there at the end of the yard.'

Alec was even less fortunate than myself, it seemed. He was also in lodgings in the town, with his wife living seventy miles away because they could not find a house locally and in the evenings, while I battled with the sea of paper 'inside' he, with a squad of men, battled 'outside', repairing holes in the walls of the workshops with sheets of second-hand galvanised zinc. Not only this place but all of postwar Britain, for those who do not remember it, was like a tattered storm-battered scarecrow.

On a cold, wet, dark evening early in 1946, I sat staring at a great heap of letters of enquiry about our plough, then took myself out and across the wet, muddy yard towards the noise of hammering.

'Alec,' I said, 'when you have a free moment, will you help me? Will you dictate to me a technical description of the plough?'

'We'll do it now if you like,' he said. 'Your office is a sight warmer than out here,' and on the way across the dark yard he said: 'I wish you'd call me Sandy. That's my name, except here. People always shorten the name Alexander and my family made it Sandy.'

'Like my family making Elizabeth into Bet,' I said.

It is easy to see now that that is where the relationship began but it was far from obvious at the time. At the time, the firm, the plough and the effort to get both under control were the thing with both of us. We were still Elizabeth and Alec in public. 'Well,' said Sandy, when we were seated side by side at my desk, 'a Treatise on the Upper Echelons of Muck-shifting.'

As the months went by, he and I shifted a great deal of muck, both inside and outside and as we did so we shifted, without knowing it, a great deal of the postwar muck in our own minds. We talked to one another a great deal during these late evenings at the office, for neither of us had anyone else to talk to and we found that our backgrounds and early lives were curiously similar. We had both been born in 1910, he in April and I in March and we had been similarly educated. We had both emerged from our adolescence into the world of the Trade Depression, but Sandy had made more of a material success of the 1930s than I had. His father, who was still alive, was a retired master blacksmith but his mother had died when he was a child, as my mother had. We had both gone to the war, Sandy in the Royal Electrical and Mechanical Engineers, for service in France, Norway and eventually India. We had both been commissioned on the recommendations of senior officers rather than by our own efforts.

In these months and, indeed, years, we saw ourselves as friendly colleagues, both interested in the development of this lively young firm and as such we argued and quarrelled, laughed and talked the war out of our systems, but this happened incidentally. Our prime interests were the firm, the plough and the plans for the future of both.

The relationship between us developed slowly and without our awareness that it was developing at all. Outside of the office and the works, we did not see each other at all and it was some months, for instance, before I knew that Sandy was not in lodgings but living with a sister and brother-in-law who owned a shop in the town. This sister, Jean, spoke to me in the street one day and after that was very kind to me and through her I met Sandy's other sister, Alice, who lived in Edinburgh. Sandy's father, known to us all as Grandpa, lived with Alice, her husband and two little girls and now if I went to Edinburgh, I had people to visit. Grandpa and I became firm friends and I have commemorated him in Old Mattha, the stonemason who figures in *My Friend Monica*.

It was through these people and not through Sandy himself that I discovered that his marriage had become something of a casualty of the war. There was no drama of unfaithfulness or adultery about it. It was a case of two people who had been pushed apart by the weather of the world, through the long absences and different experiences that the war had entailed, it seemed to me, although the family said the marriage had been a mistake from the beginning. Whatever the cause, the strain was there and there was this area of unhappiness in Sandy's life that was never mentioned between us. He and I did not talk of our immediate private lives, only of the firm, the plough, the past, the war and things that interested us, such as books and music.

During 1946 and 1947, Boss, Sandy and I brought the firm on to a sound keel and had it sailing merrily along. Our 'Treatise on the Upper Echelons of Muck-shifting' had been printed into a more elegantly-titled pamphlet with photographs of our products and we were in the export market too, for our plough was just the thing for tearing up tropical jungle and producing a tilth that would grow groundnuts, soya beans and sugar cane. And, at last, Sandy had found a house but his wife did not like the town very much, for which she was not to be blamed. It did not welcome her more than it had welcomed the rest of us. I met her on only about four occasions in all and it is one of the ironies of life that she seemed to me to bear a strong physical resemblance to Old Kirsty. No tea was taken between her and Sandy's sisters and she was not to be blamed for making frequent visits back to her home town and her people there. We all seek what little happiness and comfort we can find.

But, in retrospect, it looks as if some spirit of conspiracy were at work. We of the firm were now displaying our machines at exhibitions and agricultural shows around the country and Boss had a conviction that my presence was necessary at these affairs 'to speak to folk and take notes and things,' for he had little liking for or patience with the more social side of business.

Sandy's presence, of course, was even more necessary for he arranged the transport of our equipment and the entire display, so the day came when he and I and our crew arrived with an exhibit at Inverness and naturally my father and George came to the show, which lasted for three days, Boss deigning to attend only for the final day. Hotel rooms were scarce so Sandy and I stayed with my brother Jock and my sister-in-law, Betty, who had been married about a year before and who invited Kirsty, my father, and George for supper on our first evening and all five of my family came with us to Inverness on the final day to see the presentation to Boss of an award by the King. They were still with us on the show-ground when Sandy and the crew began to dismantle our marquee and stand.

'What a fine fellow your friend Sandy is,' my father said.

'I have never seen such a dynamo,' said my brother. 'He went up the pole of that marquee like a monkey.' George did not say anything but as soon as our equipment was loaded on to our lorries, he took Sandy off to the refreshment tent for a drink.

They were all much more interested in Sandy than in the King and the award but Sandy and I did not notice that another area of pressure was building in the weather of the world. We were much too pleased with the success of our exhibit to notice anything. We talked about it all the way south in the car except when Sandy suddenly said: 'I see now what you mean about Old Kirsty. Why do some women get such pleasure out of being shrews?'

Kirsty, when offered salad by Jock's young bride had made the response: 'You know I don't eat that rabbit's meat,' and she had made a few more remarks of similar gracelessness that had embarrassed me. It is one thing to joke with a friend about a trying member of one's family but it is another to have her be trying in his presence. If I made any reply to his question, I do not remember it. We returned to talk of our success at the show.

My father wrote to me every Sunday, the letters arrived on my desk every Tuesday morning and after the Inverness visit they always contained a few words such as: 'Give my regards to your friend Sandy,' so I began to put the letters on Sandy's desk along with the other opened mail for his attention.

Shortly after this time, there came a small crisis. My landlady decided to go to live with her married daughter so my fellow-

70

boarder and I had to find other places. I now found a room in a bungalow owned by an elderly spinster of witch-like aspect, a room which I would never have taken if I could have found any other and the lady lived up to her aspect. She personified the furtive suspicion of the town and her most disconcerting habit was to tiptoe round the outside of the house on a Sunday when I was reading in my room and peer in through the window. It was unspeakably macabre to feel that peering presence and look up to see the dark eyes and wind-blown grey hair beyond the lace curtain and it was very irritating, every time I came back to my room, to be aware that all my possessions in drawers and wardrobe had been turned over and minutely examined. At the end of two months, I arrived in the office one morning in a blind fury. 'To hell with that room, that woman and this whole town!' I said. 'I'm clearing out.'

'We can't let that happen, can we, Toots?' Sandy said to my typist. 'This place would fall apart,' and after her lunch-hour, Toots came to me and said: 'Mr Alec was asking me about lodgings and I asked my mother and she said to tell you she knows nothing about keeping lodgers but now my brother's in the Army there's his room at our place and you'd be welcome.' That evening, I walked with Toots to her home on the outskirts of the town and met her parents who became my friends Teenie and Andrew. The welcome was the thing. It was real and warm and there were no lace curtains at the windows, only long chintz ones that were drawn in the evenings.

Teenie and Andrew were of farming stock, Andrew was a farm worker and they made me a member of their gay happy family which was made up of Toots and her younger sister and the boy who was in the Army. Teenie had been brought up on a farm on the outskirts of the town and knew the backgrounds of all the townspeople and when I told her of my macabre stay with the witch in the bungalow, she rendered the whole ex-perience comical when she said: 'I'm not surprised. Her mother was aye known as Keyhole Kate.'

Andrew was a devoted husband and father who sat by the fire in the evenings, laughing and joking with his daughters or reading his newspaper. His speech was the most graphic and picturesque I have ever heard. One of the girls would do some-thing silly and he would say: 'Ye're that stupid ye'd break the heart o' a cheeny dug,' or one of them would leave open the

71

door between kitchen and living-room and be told: 'Shut that door! There's a draught like a stepmother's breath.'

It was Sandy who first addressed my typist, Lisbeth as Toots and she herself adopted the nickname by signing messages she took for him and me as Toots. She hero-worshipped Sandy, was tremendously enthusiastic about the firm and her work and when I became an adopted member of her family, I discovered that she had been reporting over the supper table each evening some of the office activity of the day. I had not been in the house for a week when Andrew greeted me at supper with the words: 'Well, did you and Mr Alec get through the day without a barney?'

'Barneys' in the office between Sandy and myself were fairly frequent and very uninhibited. Fists were banged on desks and piles of papers were thrown in the course of them and Toots had been entertaining her family with blow-by-blow descriptions, so that although her parents had never met Mr Alec any more than they had met me before they offered me a room in their home, he and I were linked in their minds as if we were two comedians, like Laurel and Hardy. And I think it is fair to assume that this link was present in minds other than those of Teenie and Andrew. After all, Toots was not the only worker in the firm with a family to amuse in the long winter evenings. There was a climate of opinion and climates exert pressures.

By the time I went to stay with Teenie and Andrew, the office was fully under control with two other girls in addition to Lisbeth working there and now that I had a pleasant place to spend my evenings, I no longer worked overtime. Early in September of 1948, the firm was to be visited by the managing director of a new company that was being established for the importation of machinery into the West Indies. The company was interested in our products and Boss said: 'I have to go to Glasgow on Friday. You two show him round and tell him what he wants to know.' This was quite usual – Boss was less interested in his inventions than in the inventions that he was going to invent – so on the Friday morning I went to the office an hour early to get the mail out of the way before the visitor arrived. I had been there for less than five minutes when Sandy arrived with a suitcase which he dumped in a corner.

'Going on holiday?' I asked in my bright lightsome way.

'You could call it that. I've left.'

'Left?'

'That house. I'm never going back,' and he went slamming out into the workshops.

It was the first time he had ever spoken to me of his home or his marriage. I cannot remember what my thoughts were or if I thought at all but the girls came in, the rush of pay-day began, routine took over and shortly before ten our visitor arrived by taxi from the local station. He was an English ex-Army officer, very interested in all we had to show and tell him. We gave him lunch at the local hotel, came back to the works to spend the afternoon and in the early evening, Sandy offered to drive him to his Edinburgh hotel. He invited us to have dinner with him, in the course of which he told us that as well as arranging agencies for machinery, he was recruiting staff. His principal concern was to find a well-qualified engineer. It was obvious that he was more than interested in Sandy and when we left the hotel I was conscious of a bleak, desolate sense of disintegration which kept me silent until the lights of the city were left behind. Then I spoke.

'That bloke is a Caribbean pirate. He would pinch you from Boss at the drop of a hat.'

'I know,' Sandy said and pulled the car into the side of the quiet road, 'and I am going to drop the hat. I am going to meet him again next week.'

'You'll go to the West Indies?' I remembered his joke of the morning when I was in a fury about my witch-like landlady. 'The firm will fall apart.'

'It will survive.'

I realised that I and not the firm was falling apart. I was recognising that three years of close friendship, of working for a common cause, of fearless, uninhibited self-expression were coalescing in these seconds into a feeling stronger than anything I had ever felt before for any other person.

'I have to clear out,' he was saying, 'because of you as much as for myself. In the heat of the battle last night, you were named as the Other Woman. Once a name like that has been given, even in private in the middle of the night, it has a way of sticking.'

'And am I the Other Woman?' I asked.

I admit to being slow, at times, to recognise facts but I claim

73

that once I have recognised them, I can be fairly quick to act on them.

'You could say that.'

'Then that's settled,' I said. 'Do you mind if I horn in on your meeting with that pirate next week? He said he wanted an office manager.'

'You are out of your mind! She'll never hear of a divorce!'

'And I won't hear of us separating,' I said.

During the weekend, we told Boss of our intentions. He was a son of the town and was not to be blamed for being, first, morally outraged and going from there into anger at the falling apart of the organisation of his firm. He was a man, I think, who had more sympathy with machines than he had with human beings and the upshot of the interview was that Sandy and I resigned more or less on the spot. We then met the 'pirate' and turned him into our Managing Director in the course of a short interview, after which we faced Grandpa, Alice and her husband and Jean and her husband at Alice's home. Society was less permissive in those days but once the initial shock was over, all five were pleased more than anything and now Sandy and I set off for The Colony.

My father and George did not know, until we told them at this time, that Sandy was married and my father, like Sandy's family was shocked at first but soon bowed and with grace to the inevitable. 'You are thirty-eight and old enough to know what you are doing,' he told me in one part of the harvest field while George and Sandy stooked corn in another, 'but there are two things you must do if you want my blessing on this. When Sandy married, he undertook to provide for the woman he married and now it is the duty of both of you to see that she is provided for. I have told Sandy this and now I am telling you. And the other thing is between you and me. You have decided what you are going to do and I want you to do it the very best you can and never let it go wrong.'

'You can take off your policeman's face,' I told him. 'She will be provided for and Sandy and I will never go wrong.'

George made no comment of any kind until after my father had gone down the hill to the village in the evening and then the comment was George-oblique. As soon as Sandy and I had arrived at The Colony, he had sent his housekeeper home on a three-day holiday. The woman was accustomed to my taking

74

over the household when I came home. When the three of us were seated around the supper table, George bent a shrewd eye on me and asked: 'Do you mind on Mick the Ditcher?' Sandy claimed afterwards that after these words were spoken, he heard me say to him: 'Wait for it!' as clearly as if I had said the words aloud. What I did say aloud was: 'Only just, George. He was killed early in the First War, wasn't he?'

'Aye. He ran away from his wife, you know. Left her in Ireland and came over here. He told me once that he wouldn't put up with any wife who wouldn't get up in the morning to make his breakfast. It is the wee things that count. Is there any more of that soup you made? Sandy and I have been working.'

In the ten years that Sandy and I spent together, there were few mornings when I did not say: 'I must get up and make the breakfast,' or he did not say: 'What about getting up and making the breakfast?' in our tropical homes with staffs of servants who made the breakfast and all the other meals.

My only worry in this whole strange, new unexpected thing that had happened to me was that Teenie and Andrew would react with disapproval and show me the door, but while Sandy and I rushed about to Edinburgh, Ross-shire and the Passport Office in Glasgow, they welcomed me home in the evenings as if nothing had happened. At the end of a hectic week, I paid for my lodging and said to Teenie: 'If you want me to leave, Teenie, just say. I'll understand.'

'Who said anything about leaving? You are welcome for as long as you like.'

'You know what has happened?'

'I know what's my business. So does Andrew. This is our house and you are welcome in it.'

'You must be the only people around here who aren't scandalised,' I said after I had told her in detail of our plans.

'Scandalised, are they? It would be a sight better if they'd look to their own firesides instead of shoving their sins on to other folk. Folk that are miserable like to make misery and they'll do it if you let them. Just don't you let them. Your life is your own business. Here, when Andrew comes home tonight, we'll take my sewing-machine up to your room. You're real good at the dressmaking and you'll make yourself some nice cotton frocks. You can't go to that hot country in these tweed costumes of yours.'

At the end of two weeks, Sandy had left by air for Jamaica but passages were difficult to obtain and I had to wait for a further three weeks, during which time I made cotton frocks with the help of Teenie's sewing-machine. While I sewed, I thought long and carefully about what had happened, what I was doing with my life and I could not see and still do not see what good there would have been for anyone in changing my course. If I would damage anyone, it would be only myself and time was to prove that there was to be no damage even to me. I did not know it at the time but I was embarking upon what was to be the most enriching relationship of my life, other than my relationships with the members of my family, but it seems to me that my only conscious positive action was the moment of embarkation when I said: 'Then that's settled.' The point of embarkation was reached without any conscious will on my part. I had been brought to that point by the weather of the world, by the world event of war, by the nature of its aftermath, by the employment I had taken, by the hostile environment around me.

I said in an earlier chapter that to write autobiography was beyond my powers and it is certainly much easier to write fiction. It was simple to transmute this time of my life into Janet's immediate recognition of Twice as somebody important to her. In actual life, this is not what happened. I made no immediate recognition of Sandy nor did I set out to 'get my man'. I did not *consciously* recognise or set out, that is and this is another matter.

When I first met Sandy, I would probably have said, had I been asked, that he was 'not my type'. I would have said that I liked tall men, like those of my family and not stocky men of little more than my own height who were going prematurely bald. I would have said that I liked farming men like my father and uncle or intellectual men like my brother, not highly practical, very oily engineers. And I would probably have said also that, having come through six years of war beset with emotional entanglements like snares at every step, I was not now going to make a fool of myself at the age of thirty-five. And, although I would not have said this aloud, my plans were to turn in an honest day's work in this job I had taken and retire in the evenings to my peaceful lodgings to try to resurrect my desire to write. It has been shown that the plans for peaceful lodgings did not materialise and that conditions were not conducive to trying to revive any talent I might have, while the demands of the firm satisfied to some extent the desire to be constructive.

What makes the writing of autobiography so difficult in my view is the very slight knowledge that, with the best will in the world, one can attain of oneself. By hindsight, considering later events, I think it possible that, without being conscious of what I was doing, I did recognise something that I needed in Sandy and something I could give to him and set out to 'get my man'. There was that first moment when I had thought that he was either ill or unhappy, but after a few days' experience of his furious energy, it seemed obvious that he was not ill but the unhappiness was undoubtedly there and showed in unguarded moments. I think it is instinctive with most of us to try to cure or to alleviate unhappiness if we can and I may have obeyed this instinct without my own awareness.

But apart from any action of Sandy's or mine, conscious or unconscious, I think that there was an outside force at work. We had emerged, with the rest of the world, from six years of hatred and destruction and in our particular case we had arrived in a bleak loveless little town. I think what happened to us has been put into words by the painter Vincent van Gogh in a letter to his brother: 'By and by I began to love my fellow-men again, myself included, and more and more my heart and soul revived, that for a time through all kinds of great misery had been withered, blighted and stricken.' As for the weather of the world, here is van Gogh again in another letter: 'If life were as simple and things as little complicated as Goody Goody's story, or the hackneyed sermon of the average clergyman, it would not be so very difficult to make one's way. But it is not so and things are infinitely more complicated, and right and wrong do not stand separately, any more than black and white do in nature.'

And even in this long chapter I have not recorded all the complications. There were my memories of my shrewish stepmother, Kirsty and my experience of the misery she could create. And George was part of what happened too. George seems to have a part in most things I do and it was he who said to me, when I was fourteen years old, in the privacy of the stable after Kirsty had made a scene in the kitchen: 'Marriages are made in Heaven, they tell me, so we can't expect much of a wee town called Kilsyth.' Need I mention that my father and Kirsty had been married in Kilsyth?

Sandy's and my marriage was not made anywhere on earth but it did not 'go wrong' and this, I think, is the best that can be said of any marriage, legal or common law. But I must not end a chapter on the word 'law'. George would not like that word to be given such importance for one of his most frequently spoken dicta was: 'There would be no need for the law at all if people behaved right and reasonable to one another.'

Chapter 8

There are many quotations from the Bible in your books. Are you a religious person?
I believe that God is love and that hatred is the Devil.

To expand this short answer, I ought to define what I mean by 'love' but I find it almost impossible to define. In my mind I have only a faint adumbration of a concept of pure, illimitable, eternal goodness, a goodness that would not because it cannot conceive the desire to hate or destroy, a goodness incapable of harbouring any of the motives which govern the human 'self'. It is a huge completeness that is willing to be absorbed by all of us, to become part of us and thus make us all part of one another.

That I and indeed I think all of us who have tried to look inside ourselves should have this awareness of something infinitely greater, finer and more mysterious than we can define is all the proof that I need that what we call God exists. If an idea takes deep and persistent root in the race mind, there is something in that idea and the concept of the mysterious indefinable 'something out there beyond reach' is as old as the recorded history of the human race.

I am not a member of any church, Christian or otherwise, but I find that the prophets of the Old Testament, Christ, and those who have chronicled them have been able to put into words better than I can many ideas in which I believe. As a writer, I always try for the best words I can find to say what I want to say and I see no shame in borrowing from better users of words than myself, provided I acknowledge that the words are borrowed.

I regard Jesus Christ not as a metaphysical figure but as a historic personage who was, as we say, 'born before his time'. The barbarous world into which he was born was not ready for his philosophy and it says little for the human capability for progress that, now, nearly two thousand years later, we have developed so little spiritually that we are still not ready for that philosophy. It is far too good for us and down the ages, too, it has been corrupted by the power to corrupt that seems to be inherent in the human race.

We all know, especially we who live in villages and small communities, how gossip travelling from mouth to mouth can distort the truth out of all recognition and through time the simple message of Christ that we love one another has been distorted to a terrifying degree. At the time when the present troubles in Northern Ireland began, I had a conversation with a minister of the Presbyterian Church in the course of which I asked him how the Reverend Ian Paisley could reconcile his behaviour with his position as a churchman and the minister replied: 'He is not a bad man. It is just that he hates the Catholics.' Can there be a more complete distortion of the simple message than this distortion to the degree when a 'man of God' can be accused of hatred and condoned in hatred by another 'man of God'?

My belief in God, in some power better and greater than ourselves, does not conflict with the theory of evolution for my belief is that we did not come from God so much as that we are going towards God. I believe that, in the beginning, the creative force was there but I also believe, as the scientists tell us, that we creatures who inhabit the earth came to birth in a primitive form where the sea met the land and I believe that, in that very moment of being born, hatred too was born. The births of ourselves and the Devil, in other words, were simultaneous, for we discovered immediately that, in order to survive, we had to think only of ourselves and be ruthless of the survival of the other lives around us. There, in the primeval slime, we made our first mistake, which has been with us ever since, when we decided to fight rather than co-operate, to hate rather than love. It is this 'sin of self-love' as Shakespeare called it, which I regard as the basic evil, for out of it is born hatred and all the other minor sins.

But I am not qualified to preach a sermon although I have heard a fair number in the course of my life, especially during my young life, for I was 'brought up in the Christian faith' which meant that I was taken to church every Sunday. At my 'away homes', church was a very tedious business but at The Colony it was quite different. For one thing, we went in the trap, drawn by Dulcie, down the steep stony hill to the shore road that led to Cromarty instead of walking along the Saturday-night-soiled pavements past the drawn blinds of pubs and pawnshops.

When I was fourteen, the last of my Cameron aunts married and left home but in my younger years I was always a little puzzled by the fact that the aunt-about-the-house never came to church. I understood, of course, that someone had always to stay at home to 'look after the place' and my grandmother had given me to understand that George and I were desperately in need of church and salvation but why did Herself or Himself never stay to look after the place and give the aunts a chance of salvation?

'It is my belief,' George explained, 'that the two of themselves are getting on a bit and feel they'd better make sure o' Heaven. There's plenty o' time for Auntie Kate.'

This made me aware, in a vague way at the age of about seven, that the sin of self-love was in my grandparents in that they were seeing, firstly, to their own salvation.

George and I did not get very far with theology and religion in general.

'George, is there really Heaven up above the sky?'

'Goodness knows.'

'George, is there really God?'

'Goodness knows.'

'George, is there really the Devil?'

'Not with a tail and horns on his head but there *is* badness in the world.'

'George, does God send people to Hell to get burned for ever and ever for being bad?'

'No decent person would do such a thing to anybody.'

You will notice that my knowledge of theology and religion has developed very little between that day and this.

We heard very little in the Scottish Presbyterian Church of those days about Jesus Christ, but we heard a great deal about the God of Vengeance of the Old Testament and, somehow, in spite of all the hour-and-a-half-long sermons, George and I could never really believe in him. It is one of the more encouraging things about us humans that we find it difficult to believe with all our hearts and minds in the ugly and the evil. We are capable of the ugly and evil but we do not fundamentally believe in them as we believe in the beautiful and the good, the 'something out there beyond reach'. We turn away from the ugly and evil, often into laughter. It is said, for instance, that the Punch and Judy show is based on Pontius Pilate and Judas Iscariot and certainly, in the 1930s here in Scotland, we had a comedian called Dave Willis who used to bring the house down with his impersonation of Adolf Hitler. He used to take the stage in short leather trousers and a hat bedecked with a feather and open his song with the, for me, unforgettable words:

> *I'm a Tyrolean*
> *No' a big yin, jist a wee yin.*

In a similar way, George and I turned away from Yahweh, the God of Vengeance by re-preaching the sermons of the Hebridean minister in the privacy of our various hide-outs from my grandmother.

After the coming of what was called 'the wireless', Highland speech, like that of other districts, began to become standardised and much of the feeling went out of it. I have always thought that the pronunciation 'Wipers' conveyed much more tearful sorrow than the more correct 'Ypres' and up here during that first war there was talk of a foreign place that had the mournful name 'Gallee*poh*lee' which it took me some time to identify as the Gallipoli of the newspapers.

In the Hebridean speech, some consonants were hardened and some softened, some vowels broadened and some narrowed so that the words of Yahweh, as spoken by our minister, became '– for I the Lord thy Cod am a chealous Cod'. The resemblance in the minds of George and myself between Yahweh and the large fish hanging from the eaves of Bella Beagle the fishwife's house was often almost too much for us in church and out of church we mimicked the words of the minister and gave ourselves the relief of laughter.

It cannot be denied that, down the ages the Christian religion has been a great factor in divisiveness and it must be because of what George called the badness in the world that a gospel of love and unity should have been distorted to have this effect. I think the greatest badness in the world is that sin of self-love which dictates that each man must see himself as better, richer, cleverer or even more Christian than his fellows. Cromarty, until about 1920, when the fishing industry moved away from the town, was divided into two factions, those who lived by the sea and those who lived by the land. The fisher people believed that they were closer to God because Christ had found his friends among the fishermen of Galilee and the farming people believed that they were closer to God because God had placed Adam and Eve in a garden. The schoolchildren fought physical battles over this issue in the playgrounds of the school and their parents fought over the issue in the pubs.

We of the Cameron family did not fight in playgrounds or pubs but my grandparents and parents were not immune from this folly. On Friday evenings, when I returned from my visits to the fishertown, I had to wash with carbolic soap before I came into the house and throughout supper there would be sniffings from my grandmother and remarks addressed to the air, such as: 'What in the world she sees in those dirty fishwives I'll never know.' But my grandmother was in a cleft stick over the fishwives. To stop me from visiting them, she would have had to keep me at home and she could not do that for it would mean letting that clown George go to Cromarty on his own. The race is permanently in the cleft stick of its own ambivalence.

The truth is that the people of my family, like most Highland crofters of their time, were not Christians at all, in spite of their faithful church-going. Their true religion, although they would never have admitted it, was something far older than Christianity, much more deeply rooted in them and more primitive and pagan. Their true gods were the sun, the moon, the earth and the weather of the seasons. I have attended a number of religious services of many kinds in my time but I have never at any of them been aware of such unity in awe, such devout and mystic silence as reigned in The Colony kitchen while the Old Year ticked out its dying moments and the New Year was born with the arrival of our First Foot, the dark-haired neighbour who brought us gifts of luck for the year that was opening before us. These symbolic gifts were handled with a reverence deeper than I ever saw in Cromarty church on Sunday. The placing of the gift lump of coal or wood on the fire, the placing of the gift shortbread and bottle of whisky on the dresser were the true acts of worship that my family made and when the day in spring came when my grandfather looked at the sky, sniffed the wind, kicked a clod of earth and said: 'We'll start sowing the corn,' it was as if a peal of bells were ringing out over The Colony hill.

I think their reaction to the religion preached in church was one of scepticism tempered by a canny conforming 'just to be on the safe side'. Certainly, during the 1930s, when my brother and I, home on holiday, rebelled about attending church, my father said: 'It may not do you any good but it won't do you any harm,' and then the mild blackmail: 'Maybe you'll come just to please me,' and to please him, we went, but we were both aware that we were at church only to reinforce our father's image of himself as a respectable citizen.

This respectable citizen with the gold watch-chain across his waistcoat was not the real man and neither was the immaculately uniformed policeman. The real Duncan Cameron was the man in the old clothes and battered hat standing on top of the hill with his hand on the mane of a horse while he looked away to the hills or the man in the garden, snipping away with his shears, as he turned a big privet bush into a green statue of the horse.

During his thirty-two years in the Lowlands in the police service, my father had become imbued with some of the values and beliefs of urban industrial society but when some issue that was of deep importance to him cropped up, he reverted to the old values and judgements of the crofting community. During the First World War, there was a local scandal when a young woman became pregnant with an illegitimate child. Someone said in my grandmother's hearing that she was a 'bad girl' and I remember Herself at her tallest and most stern saying: 'Hold your wicked tongue! Bad girls don't *have* babies.' A similar thing happened during the Second World War when a local girl was sent home, pregnant, from one of the services. When I joined the Air Force, I had got rid of most of my clothes but an elaborate alabaster buckle to which a number of different-coloured suede belts could be fixed and which had been a feature of various outfits was shipped home among the books and the few things I wanted to keep. When I came home on leave, I got off the bus in the middle of the village to be met by my father and the pregnant girl, the elaborate alabaster buckle prominent upon her distended stomach.

'Why did you go giving away that buckle of mine?' I asked my father when we were inside the house.

'You don't need it,' he said, 'but the lassie needs something to show people she has friends,' and Old Kirsty, who naturally regarded the girl as a disgrace, knew from his tone that it would be better to make no comment.

At The Colony, when the Sunday church service was over, and the Sunday clothes hung up thankfully for another week, the real religion of the family took charge, with my grandmother as the high priestess. Early on Monday morning, she went into action. To the aunt-about-the-house it would be: 'You can unpick that tweed skirt that Mary sent home to me. I don't like it but it will make fine wee trousers for the Ferguson twins,' and then: 'George, when you open the tattie pit tomorrow, fill three bags and take them down to Mrs Williamson. That man of hers is good for nothing but making bairns.' And to me: 'And don't you go prowling away up the moor. I want you to take a few eggs and a bittie butter down to old Mrs Macleod in the village.'

Mrs Macleod, by the way, had her cottage, the Lloyd George pension and the most beautiful china I had ever seen on the shelves of her dresser. There were cups, saucers and plates that were all 'presents' from somewhere and one was allowed to choose the china that one would use, so that one could have tea out of a cup that was a present from Rothesay, set on a saucer that was a present from Stirling and eat a biscuit from a plate that was a present from Galashiels.

But there was one house to which I frequently had to carry a basket of scones and oatcakes under the instruction: 'Now, don't you dare to eat a bite in that house. Say no thank you and that I said you were to hurry home. Mrs Campbell has too many mouths to feed to put anything into yours.' The 'love one another' of this primitive religion took a very practical form.

The priestesses – it was a matriarchal religion – were also the midwives and veterinarians of their districts and my grandmother brought a little ancient mysticism into such services by way of inducing some respect for the valuable rites she celebrated when tending a woman in childbirth or a sick animal. There was a local superstition that she was a witch and she fostered this rather than otherwise but George and my father explained to me fairly early in my life that she was no witch, but only a little cleverer, more cunning and more observant than most of the people around her, characteristics common, I suspect, to the priests and priestesses of all religions, primitive or otherwise.

I remember a dark evening around the Christmas period

during the First World War when the owl that lived among the tall trees above the well began to hoot just outside the house. This often happened. The owl came in close to the steading after dark to hunt mice but on this evening my grandmother said: 'Seven times. George, go out and yoke the trap. Belle, get my things. That will be Mrs Ferguson,' and off she went, to arrive home early the next morning after delivering the Ferguson twins. Now, we were all accustomed to the owl hooting around the house, it may have hooted seven times or seventy but she said seven and it was natural to believe her and it was natural too to forget that she had seen Mrs Ferguson only a day or two before and was so experienced that she could estimate the time of a birth within a few hours.

I remember, too, the Sunday afternoon when George and I accompanied her on foot across the moor to the croft of a neighbour who had had a young mare serviced by an expensive stallion. The service had cost some astronomical sum of about ten pounds and it was of great importance to know as early as possible if the mare was in foal. In the little stable, Granny walked round the animal, looking at her from every angle, rubbing her hands over the back and belly, crooning the while in Gaelic. She was bilingual but would not teach the 'old tongue' to any of us and spoke it only to animals and a few old friends of her own age. Then she asked our neighbour to bring her a white bowl filled with water fresh from the spring with a silver sixpence lying at the bottom of the bowl and when this was brought she poured a few drops of the water into the mare's ear, still crooning softly in Gaelic. A moment later, she turned to our neighbour and said: 'You are all right, Sandy. She is in foal,' and sure enough, the mare was in foal.

My father and I often talked of this in later years and his theory was that had the mare not been in foal she would have shaken herself violently at the shock of the icy water in her ear but that, being in foal, she probably responded less violently, perhaps shaking only her head, but I had not been observant enough to notice the movement of the animal. Then my father would add: 'Of course, you have to remember those hands of hers. For some things, it was as if she had eyes in her finger-ends. And then she was an old woman who had seen a lot of birth and death and a young mare, to her, was like a young woman.' But the trappings of the high priestess were there in the white

86

bowl, the piece of silver and the mystic intimate crooning in the old tongue which was unfamiliar to the rest of us. She could mount a most convincing performance.

She had a deep intimacy with the earth, with growing things, with birds and animals and with the weather and her attitude to the earth and the weather, in particular, used to make me think of the commandment given to Moses: 'Honour thy father and thy mother that thy days may be long upon the land—' She honoured the earth and the weather as the parents upon whom she depended for nurture.

My father, the gardener, brought home to her from the Lowlands cuttings of geraniums which grew in pots on the broad windowsill of the kitchen and in summer, when they were flowering red, pink and white, her long day began shortly after dawn with her standing at the window, looking out at the sky, the garden and the trees of the moor beyond while the tips of her fingers played among the earth of the geranium pots. I think this was her true form of prayer and not the 'Our Father which art in Heaven' on Sundays, when she wore her best hat and her black gloves. Her religion was in her kinship with people, all living things, the sky and especially the earth and it strikes me now that I am one of the many children she delivered at birth. The longest journey she ever made away from The Colony was when she came to Renton to be with my mother at my birth and perhaps I ought to remember those hands of hers. They would have been the first hands to touch me and perhaps they gave me something of her 'primitive' religion. I am certainly an incurable dabbler in the earth; I have more interest in people and their happiness than in trying to save my own soul through orthodox religion but I wish she had endowed me with more of her wisdom. No. I take back that last. I must try to learn my own wisdom, be grateful for what talent I have been given and hope to achieve the contentment which made The Colony the place it was.

I come of a lawless, cattle-stealing, claymore-waving ancestry but in my father these traits were perforce subdued by his police service. He had a profound respect for the law and tended at times, indeed, to confuse it with morality but no such confusion ever entered the mind of George.

My father was very much aware of his parental responsibility and especially after the death of our mother he was at great pains to bring up my brother and me to the best of his ability. I think it remarkable and I am sure that those who remember the attitudes to sex of 1923 will agree with me, that when I was thirteen, he took me for a walk one Sunday afternoon and informed me clearly and with no salacious self-consciousness or embarrassment of the 'facts of life'. As he saw it, my mother was no longer present to look after me in this way, the matter was his responsibility and he carried it through. I had seen calvings and foalings at The Colony by this time and from there he moved on to what I myself could expect, ending with the words: 'I don't want you to be afraid. The thing is quite normal,' which led to a small private joke between him and me. Always a late developer, I was nearly seventeen before menstruation began and shortly after my sixteenth birthday, I took *him* for a walk one Sunday afternoon and opened the conversation with: 'Look here, I am not normal.' Thereafter, when Old Kirsty was protesting loudly about some of my unnatural goings-on, he used to wink at me behind her back and say: 'The trouble with you is that you are not normal.'

In contrast with my father, George did not believe in bringing people up but in helping them to grow. My father partook of the general family attitude that George was a clown and did not come to understand, until long after we were grown up, that George had profoundly influenced my brother and myself. This was not deliberate on George's part. It simply came about because he was the man he was.

My father kept to the conventional rules of morality but George constructed his own morality as he went along and his chief rule was that he would not interfere in the morals of anyone else, expected no one to interfere in his morals, an arrangement which worked very satisfactorily. My father upheld the law but George upheld it only when he considered it fair and reasonable and nobody was ever clever enough to catch him when he broke it. Thus one has the comic picture of two devoted brothers, one chasing poachers in the Lowlands while the other was poaching right, left and centre in the Highlands; one seeing that premises licensed to sell liquor closed at the proper time in the Lowlands while the other was making liquor in an illicit still in the Highlands. My father, until the end of his life, never knew half of the 'lawlessness' of George and he is not to be scorned for that, for my cunning grandmother, on the spot,

88

never knew the half of it either. Or did she know and condone it? She had little use for the law herself beyond the fact that my father earned an income from its upholding. But least of all did anyone in the family suspect that George, 'that clown that spends half his time making a fool of himself with the bairns', could be affecting my brother and me and the effects did not show until long after our childhood, when my father, a deep blue Tory, discovered that his son was voting Labour and that his daughter was prepared to 'run away' with a man she could not marry.

I wish to mark the fact that I am not blaming George for the flaws in our characters. I am merely pointing out that, but for him, we might have been different, perhaps better, although I take leave to believe that, without his influence, we might have been a great deal worse.

My father used to treat us to homilies occasionally about things like avoiding debt and treating other people as we would like them to treat us but George did not indulge in homilies. He simply said and did things, in the ordinary course of events, that stayed with us and became part of our thinking. At the age of about nine, I went with him to a ploughing match in a field that belonged to a 'gentleman farmer' named Mackenzie and there we met a new member of the organising committee who was encountering George for the first time. 'I am told you are one of the best ploughmen and have one of the best plough pairs in the district, Mr Cameron,' he said. 'Why are you not entered?'

'I come to ploughing matches to see my friends,' George replied quietly, 'not to work Mackenzie's ground for him.' He made one see all round his view of ploughing matches. He wanted them to be friendly affairs, he did not approve of a rich man having his land ploughed more or less gratis and he had no interest in competing with his neighbours. But when one of our neighbours became ill in the spring, it was George and his plough pair that turned over his land for him.

I used to be annoyed that I could not hoe turnips as well as he could. No matter how hard I tried, I either took out too many plants or too few and my row never looked as elegantly finished as his did. At this time, I did not know that few people could hoe as well as he could.

'Never mind,' he would tell me. 'You don't have to be as good

89

as anybody else or better than anybody else as long as you are doing your best and that row of yours is just fine. We are getting on grand. Another three days and we'll be done.'

Do you wonder that Kirsty's Dux Medal had no importance for me?

During the First World War, I was looking out of the little back window of the house across the dark firth one night when the black starry sky was suddenly rent this way and that with long shafts of white light. Frightened, I ran through to the kitchen and everybody came back with me to the window. My grandparents and my aunt were frightened too, I could feel it, but George said: 'Searchlights. The ships have them.' Relieved, the others went back to the kitchen fire but George put his hand on my shoulder and said: 'I don't like them either. They spoil the sky.' I have often wondered if this was the beginning of my dislike for neon signs, fireworks and all such spoilers of the sky.

George did not like to hurt anybody or anything that could be hurt. This is why the idea of him as a real soldier, killing men, is ludicrous and perhaps this is why the Second World War had such a traumatic effect on me. In the economy of The Colony, the vermin such as mice, rats, rabbits, weasels and hoodie crows had to be killed. George saw the necessity for this and with the help of Angus the ferret and the dogs, we dealt with the mice and rats while the gun came into play against the weasels and hoodie crows. He was a deadly shot with his double-barrelled gun and admitted to me much later in life that he had been a member of his regiment's marksman team.

It occurs to me that I may be portraying George as a prodigy who did everything with excellence but this was not so. He could do only a few simple things but he did them surpassingly well and there was one difficult thing which he did supremely well, which was living.

When vermin-killing, he had a soft spot for the rabbits which invaded the fields and ate the young corn and he shot as few as he could get away with and would never eat my grand-mother's excellent rabbit stew, but he could deal death to the mice and rats that spoiled the oats so that the horses would not eat them and to the weasels and hoodie crows that preyed upon the young chickens and ducklings. But he would never shoot woodpigeons or the beautiful pheasants and partridges although

My parents – on the left, my mother aged twenty-seven, right, my father aged thirty-one

My brother Jock as an Ordinary Seaman in 1939

The author

*The author as
Flight Officer
(Intelligence)
WAAF, 1945*

my grandmother often expressed a wish for a brace for the pot. I suppose it was at the early age when he taught me to stand to his left and a little behind him when we were out with the gun that he also taught me that he frequently 'missed'. He would bring down the two weasels in the march dyke, the hoodie crow flying over the old quarry and then say: 'Now we'll try for that brace of partridges Herself wants.' Then, beyond the tall trees above the well, out of sight of the house, he would say: 'Well, which ones?' and I would point to two little fir cones, one on our left, one on our right, high against the sky, the two barrels would crack and down would come the cones. Back at the house, he would break the gun, start to clean it and say to my grandmother: 'We fired at a pair o' partridges above the well but we missed.'

'A fine thing and cartridges such a terrible price!' she would say scornfully. (It occurs to me now that I have given the words: 'Cartridges such a terrible price', to Angus in *Camerons on the Hills*.)

George taught me the most important thing of all when I was seven years old. It was summer and we were bringing the last sheaves of corn into the barn from the stackyard which would soon be filled again with the sheaves of the new crop. We were working Angus and the dogs properly, as laid down by my grandmother, with the ferret net round the half-stack, enclosing George, me, Angus and the dogs. Angus was inside the stack, bolting the rats which the dogs killed when they came out into the netted enclosure. A half-grown rat bolted out at my feet, the dogs were busy and, afraid that it would get through the net, on impulse I picked it up to throw it to the dogs. It turned its head and fixed its filthy, green-moulded teeth in my left fore-finger, just at the side of the nail. I yelled, the rat dangling from the finger and George said: 'The dirty boogger!' He tore it off, a little piece of my finger clenched between its teeth, brained it on the toe-cap of his boot and ran me down to the house where my grandmother got busy on the wound.

I had a very painful finger although all I have to show for it now is an almost invisible little scar and when the wound had been cleaned and bandaged and I had stopped crying, I said: 'I *hate* rats! I *hate* them, *hate* them! I'll *always* hate them!' The next day, in the stable, George said: 'You said a very bad word yesterday when the rat bit you.' 'I did *not!*' I argued. 'It was *you* that said dirty boogger.'

My grandmother was always scolding George for saying bad words like boogger and devil and damn.

'You said far worse,' he told me, 'and you weren't even angry at the time and your finger was bandaged and not so sore any more. You said *hate.*' He spoke the word in an emphasised undertone, as if it were too dreadful to speak aloud. 'I never thought to hear you use that word.'

'It's a bad word, George?'

'The worst word in the whole wide world, far worse than boogger or devil or shit or any of them. It's far worse than damn, even.'

'Why?'

'Ach, boogger and devil and shit are just words that don't mean anything and damn is just stupid because nobody can damn anybody, but hate is something you can do and it is a very bad thing to do and a bad word to say.'

These words may not be exactly as spoken but the meaning I convey is exact and many many years later, I heard similar words spoken by him to Shona as a small child. She had been out to tea and said: 'The cake had crystallised cherries in it. I hate crystallised cherries.'

'You don't hate crystallised cherries, Shona,' George said. 'You just don't like the taste of them.'

Hate to George was a bad word and hatred the badness in the world, the Devil without horns or tail and it was at The Colony, in the stable, (a not inappropriate place) that he laid the foundation stone of what I call my religion.

Chapter 9

Do you keep notebooks and diaries and write at regular hours?
No.

Most writers seem to be, from what I have heard and read, creatures of habit. I certainly am and during the 1930s I developed a habit of writing when I got the chance.

I have consistently described my employment during that period as uninteresting but it strikes me now that, perhaps, from a socio-historic point of view, some of my positions were of some minor interest. In some situations, I was really an extension of the office of the King's Proctor, for several of the women who employed me were between divorce and re-marriage, going through the period between the decree nisi and the decree absolute, when they were required to conduct themselves as the law deemed proper. The situation did not arise for me but, in theory, if the King's Proctor accused any of them of impropriety, I would be the witness for the defence. It is as well that the situation did not arise, because I should have been faced with the decision whether or not to perjure myself and my decision would have been against perjury.

I moved from one post to another fairly frequently for, once the re-marriage had been celebrated, my doubtful services were no longer required and there was always an acquaintance of my employers at the decree nisi stage who required a chaperon for the ensuing six months. It occurs to me now that mine was a form of employment to incline one to a somewhat cynical view of the public marriage vow of lifelong faithfulness as well as of the workings of the law itself.

It is a small argument in favour of my belief that nothing is totally pernicious that my type of employment gave me quite a lot of free time, but this time did not come at regular hours. It depended on my employer's whim to go and buy hats or have her hair done or go to friends for the afternoon or to spend the morning having her face massaged or, of course, to go away for the weekend, so I learned to start to write as soon as the chauffeur

93

had shut the door of the car and driven round the corner of the street.

Ernest Hemingway wrote in pencil, standing up at a chest-height desk and Henry Miller has said that he thinks it beneficial to writers to work in an uncomfortable position, but I developed the habit of writing with a fountain pen on loose sheets of paper made firm by a book underneath. As I filled each sheet, I put it under the blank sheets and I always sat either in a chair with a cushion at my back or in bed with pillows behind me so that, if by any chance I were surprised at my secret activity, the paper went behind the cushion or pillows, the pen down the spine of the book and I was ostensibly only reading the book.

In December of 1956, after returning to Jamaica from leave in this country, I decided that the time had come, aged forty-six, to make a real effort to put on paper the material that was stuffing my head. Much of this material had been written down a number of times before between 1931 and 1956 and then destroyed but I was now going to try for the final form. I decided to open with *My Friend Muriel* as already has been told.

I had always written on quarto paper when I could afford it but in Jamaica the quarto which was imported was American and a little bigger than the British size, so I scoured the house for a book big enough to act as a backing board and what I found was an atlas, of about foolscap size and an inch thick. I still write with a cushion behind me with this atlas on my knees. Its spine wore out from the grip of my left hand: I repaired it with a five-inch strip of sticky-back plastic and now, I note, the plastic has worn through where my left hand takes its grip. It is little wonder, when I think of it, for this atlas has been on my knees for many hours in the course of nearly twenty years.

I make no serious complaint about the dull employment of my earlier years, therefore, because it taught me to take interruptions in mid-sentence and go on to complete the sentence hours or days later. These were expected interruptions, because I was writing illicitly in my employer's 'time'. Expected interruptions are quite different in effect from the unexpected telephone call from a stranger or the American lady on the doormat who is on vacation and just felt she *had* to see you.

During that debauch of writing between December 1956 and

about March 1958, when I put seven novels on paper, I was running a household and had plenty of interruptions, so expected interruptions are part of my writing life.

I now live alone, which means that, in theory, I can write all day if I feel like it but theory makes no allowance for human idiosyncrasy. As I have said, I was strictly brought up in the old-fashioned Scottish tradition of housekeeping and I am only now, at sixty-four, beginning to be able to write on a Monday morning instead of doing the weekly wash. I still have a sense of sin about putting it off till Tuesday which I know to be ridiculous without my brother telling me that I am a fool to be bullied by the odd soiled dish-towel.

So I write on a pad on my knee in an armchair by a log fire, a pretty picture, but log fires do not light themselves. The day begins for me about seven in the morning when I come downstairs, make a pot of tea, carry the tray up to my bedroom and sit in bed, drinking tea and contemplating the waters of Udale Bay during one half of the year and the dark beyond the window during the other half. I am usually dressed and downstairs by eight-thirty and now the construction of the pretty picture of the writer by the log fire begins. I fetch bucket and shovel, remove the ashes of the day before, bring in logs, paper, small kindling wood, then find the matchbox is empty. I go to the kitchen drawer for the last box of matches, take off my fire-cleaning gloves and write 'matches' on the shopping-list. I am also using the last of my kindling wood and make a mental note to chop some more in the garden shed before the winter dark descends at three-thirty. When the fire is alight, I kneel on the hearth-rug looking at it, enjoying it, knowing that the rose bushes in the garden are covered with hoar frost and then I remember the birds and go to the kitchen to find some crusts and scraps of fat for the bird-table. And now, while I am standing here while the sparrows chirp at me from the roof, the starlings squawk at me from the thicket and Johnnie, my half-tame, one-legged seagull goes 'Awk-awk!' at me from his perch beside the chimney-pot, standing among all this clear frosty cleanliness, I face up to that sinister little black thing I noticed beside the bread-bin in the kitchen. There are mice in my kitchen. Mice come into my kitchen every year when the frost comes. And since I am facing up to things, I tell myself, I may as well face up to that smell in the linen cupboard upstairs. I had been hoping that it would go away but smells do not go away. They merely get worse, something I knew all the time. This is an example of the triumph of human hope over human experience.

So I open the door of the linen cupboard, shut it again and telephone my nephew who is on vacation from university to ask him to come up for a few days and cement up all the holes he can find in the outsides of my two-feet-nine-inches-thick walls. And only when he arrives do I say: 'And, Neil, there is the most awful smell in the linen cupboard.' He looks puzzled and I have to explain that I have been putting down poison in the kitchen for the mice but they have this habit of going up to the nice warm linen cupboard to die. With Neil in the house, I do little but cook for he is twenty-one, six feet tall and cannot hunt mice all day on an empty stomach. Then the fishmonger comes and we chat, then a man with a load of firewood and we chat and then a great skein of wild geese comes over to settle in Udale Bay which I watch with delight and Johnnie Seagull watches with indignation. And the crocus and snowdrop spears are poking through the frozen earth. I can spend a lot of time looking at snowdrop and crocus spears.

For days, weeks, months at a time, I employ myself at anything as long as it is not writing. I have hedged myself about with resistances to writing such as a house and garden to keep on my own without help. I could afford to pay for help in the house but I would not write in the time saved anyway. I am so habitually secretive a writer that, to do it at all, I have to be alone behind a closed door.

Until fairly recently, I thought that these resistances were accidents thrust upon me by life, telling myself I had to have a roof over my head and could not look out of my windows on to a wilderness of weeds, but all that was mere self-deception. It is only fairly recently that I have found, I think, the explanation as to why, as a writer, I spend so much time resisting the desire to write. The extraordinary thing is that the desire is there and it is the desire I am resisting.

Yet, I feel guilty when I am not writing, I feel that I am letting my publishers down, that I have no right to be doing housekeeping and gardening that I could pay people to do for me, but nothing makes me change my ways. I think that the explanation is that the essential part of the writing is done while I am cooking, looking at snowdrop spears and talking to Johnnie

Seagull about the wild geese. In a way that was, until recently, subconscious, I idle about doing other things until I have built up a head of steam such as I had when I put seven novels on to paper in some fifteen months. That head took thirty-four years to build, from the age of twelve to the age of forty-six but now that I know a little more about my craft and have found the form into which to put my words, I can get steam up in perhaps a year and get the novel on to paper in about three months.

This is why, I think, that the three months in the 'ideal haven' above the blue Caribbean were so sterile. I could build up no resistance there. I had nothing to do but write, which simply does not work for me and this is why, earlier, I expressed my doubts about awards, grants and financial help for writers.

When an idea becomes commonly accepted by humanity in general, I think there is always a grain of truth behind it. I would go so far as to say that there is something like a communal human-race mind, which would account for the simultaneous springing-up of the same idea in different parts of the world at the same time and the communal mental picture of the artist starving in a garret seems to me to have a grain of truth in it. What may be less familiar as an idea is my own notion that the artist creates his own garret and goes on hunger strike. I must interpolate here that I do not regard myself as an artist – I find 'artist' a very big word and the word 'genius' very much bigger – and I have not the temerity to apply the word artist to myself or the word genius to any practitioner of the arts who is still alive. I think only the centuries to come can recognise true genius and all geniuses in my view are physically dead but spiritually alive.

The artist starves in his garret because he must have the resistance of the garret and the starvation but these privations can take many forms. Proust's version of garret and resistance was the neurasthenia which he must have known he was encouraging by his extraordinary way of life and I can imagine Shakespeare telling himself that he ought to stay put somewhere and write *Hamlet* but going on tour as a strolling player none the less and coming back eventually to write the *Hamlet* we know, which is probably the play it is because he waited until the head of steam was strong enough, using the tour as a resistance against the moment when that white quill would reach the paper.

97

A writer of my acquaintance put this resistance to writing and the postponement of starting to write in another way. 'There comes the day,' she said, 'when you face the fact that God will not pick up the ballpoint.'

As I see it, we have great works like *Hamlet* and small ones like my own because Shakespeare could take in more steam in the way of understanding, compassion, observation and all the things needed to make literary steam than I can, he could also compress it harder into more power and when the moment came to let it loose, he had the ability to canalise it through the best-chosen words ever written.

And now, if you have read your Dr A. L. Rowse, you are going to tell me that Shakespeare had the help of a patron in the form of the Earl of Southampton and ask me why young modern writers should not have grants, but Dr Rowse shows little evidence of patronage in a financial sense. That Southampton was Shakespeare's patron at all is in some doubt in some quarters but the patronage that Dr Rowse causes to sound very convincing was a matter of friendship, encouragement and recognition. Indeed, had Shakespeare had no more than my minor talent, he would probably have written a novel entitled *My Friend Southampton*.

This patronage of encouragement and recognition is all the better for the writer if it can be given along with friendship, for this is what the writer really needs. I was stupid enough, at twenty-one, when my first employer discovered that I was buying a typewriter on the hire-purchase system and asked why I was doing such a thing when I could do all the writing *she* required with a pen, to reply: 'I thought I might be able to write a magazine article or two some time.'

'*You* write for magazines?' she said. 'Don't be ridiculous!' (Ridiculous as it is, it still hurts to write that down.)

It was the only time I was ever stupid enough to tell anyone except my father – I did not even tell George – that I wanted to write. I have said that I have to write against resistance of some kind but it must not be the withering sort of resistance of that woman.

I have now had published eighteen novels in the Reachfar series, four in the Jean Robertson series, five novels for young people in the Camerons series and have in course of production a picture book for young children. Some months ago, I sent the fourth and final typescript of the Jean Robertson series to my editor and went through the same agony that the agents' reading of *My Friend Muriel* had caused me all those published books and fifteen years ago. I cannot eat or sleep, I sit around the house or wander round the garden like a zombie with nausea until I am assured that what I have written is fit for publication.

I have such a close intimacy with what I write that I can make no judgement upon it and have to be told by my editor that it 'will do'. Since he came to know about this extraordinary failing of mine, he has asked me to send him three copies of my typescripts so that the novel can be read simultaneously by himself and two other readers and by Heaven knows what efforts, they manage to wade through my badly-typed scripts and give me a verdict in nine days.

We have a Mongol child in the family and I can only say that when I write a novel, I no more know that it is a novel than my sister-in-law knew, during the nine months of her pregnancy, that she was carrying a Mongol child. Such being my attitude, my amazement can be imagined when, shortly after I entered the writing world, I chanced to meet a man in his early twenties who had just had his first novel refused by the first publisher to whom he had sent it. He was very angry. 'The fools!' he said. 'I *know* I can write!' Writers come in all kinds but I may say that in my reading of the literary news during the last twelve years, I have never seen his name mentioned. (He may, of course, now be using a pseudonym.)

On the subject of diaries and notebooks, I buy a diary every year but I have never kept a notebook. The diaries are never entered up journal-fashion. I use them only for dates and times of trains or aeroplanes and for appointments I have to keep on my infrequent forays beyond the bounds of Jemimaville.

I am told and I think it is true that I have a very retentive memory for things like conversations and fashion at a certain period and my memory works by a web of association. For instance, today as I write it is the sixth of September and I can tell you that it is eleven weeks and one day since I have been further from my home than the village shop three hundred yards away, because my editor, his wife and children were the last people to drive me out by car and they stayed with me over the weekend of the longest day in the year. We went to Loch Ness so that the children could look for the Monster but they did not see it. I saw my first submarine in July of 1916 because George and I were building a new coop for my hen Chickabird and the brood of chicks that she had just brought home from her nest hidden in a whin bush on the moor. George sent me to the cartshed for a four-inch nail and on my way back, I looked down at the Cromarty Firth and saw, gliding along the surface, a replica of my four-inch nail, the head going first and the rest of the craft tailing off to a point like the nail. I called George to look at it, he told me it was a submarine and the year was 1916 because, like all good architects, he and I always inscribed our buildings with the date of their construction. As soon as he had driven the last big nail, he had a stand-easy and filled his pipe while I opened the can of black paint and dated the coop 'July 1916', in large letters and figures.

In late November and early December of 1972, I read what, to me, is an extraordinary book and I can tell you so precisely when I read it because I bought it in Boston, Massachusetts and read it during the journey home. It is called *Journal of a Novel* and was written by John Steinbeck.

Many writers have kept notebooks and Somerset Maugham published quite a thick volume which contained only a small portion of the notes of a lifetime, while Thomas Wolfe, after the completion of his novel *Of Time and the River*, documented his work on it in *The Story of a Novel*. The extraordinary thing about Steinbeck's *Journal of a Novel* is that it was written not before or after the event but concurrently with the writing of his novel *East of Eden*.

In a large notebook, on the left-hand pages, Steinbeck wrote a daily letter to his editor (some editors get things even harder than mine) and on the right-hand pages he wrote the first draft of *East of Eden*, a process which took from the twenty-ninth of January to the first of November 1951. On the left-hand pages Steinbeck not only describes the day to day activities of his household but also sets down his plans for his day's work on his novel, his thoughts about it and how he sees the next part of it unfolding and developing.

When I first read this *Journal* in 1972, my thought was that if I tried to put my thoughts about my work down in letters in this way, the novel would die on me. It would be like exposing the roots of a plant to the withering wind and frost of the world, so that it would shrivel up and die. Now, however, nearly three years later, I think I have discovered why Steinbeck could write these letters and also write his book which I could not do. Steinbeck was detached from his novel; it was something that he was building, as George and I might build a chicken coop and this may be the best, most correct and proper way to write novels. John Steinbeck did, after all, receive the Nobel Prize for Literature in 1962.

But one can only write in one's own way and my way has nothing of this detachment in it. My novels are spun like a thread out of some store of material that is inside me, they are part of me and private to me until the moment when I post the typescript to my editor. Then come the anxious days until I am told the thing 'will do' and in that moment the relief is enormous and as if an umbilical cord had been cut, the detachment is complete. From that moment onwards, I never want to have anything more to do with that novel. To read its proofs is a colossal bore as are all the other little bits and pieces and small queries and decisions about its production in book form.

There is a piece of equipment much more important to a writer than all the diaries and notebooks, and than all visual and aural memory, which Ernest Hemingway described in the course of an interview in the following unminced words: 'The most essential gift for a good writer is a built-in shock-proof shit detector. This is the writer's radar—' I think that I spent part of the twenty-six years between 1931, when I first put pen to paper and 1957, when I decided to type up *My Friend Muriel*, unconsciously developing my radar system. My bonfires of the years were detected ****.

It is very easy, when one sets sail on the course of a novel, to let the head of steam get out of control, to let it rush up through the siren to make a loud bombastic noise, instead of canalising it into the feed-pipes of the engines that keep the ship of the novel sailing smoothly and directly on course.

The typewriter is a wonderful **** detector. Now, most machines and I have nothing in common. I am afraid of them and they know it. I would rather drive twenty-five live horses than a twenty-five-horse-power car, if there is such a thing. I do not drive a car, have given up driving my electric sewing-machine and pay other people to sew, I plug in my washing-machine, then shut the door on it and let it do its worst. I have an electric beater and liquidiser which terrifies me and sometimes my typewriter, of which I am not really scared, ups and defies me. It goes and jams itself because I have leaned on some of its knobs or levers by mistake, so I lean all over it until I happen to lean on the bit that unjams it. But it is a wonderful final **** detector. A passage that flowed from the pen like a stream of purple-tinted honey that would act as a love-potion on any reader, when clicked into cold, black print on white by the typewriter, suddenly becomes a sticky mess, buzzing with bluebottle flies. Because of this invaluable endowment, I love my typewriter.

While I am on the subject of machines, I would remind you that Sandy was an engineer to the backbone. He did not prefer machines to people but regarded them *as* people, secondary sorts of people with personalities of their own and refreshingly more predictable than the real thing. And they were all female. We did not stay long with the firm we had joined in the West Indies because Sandy said it turned him into a 'ten-per-cent Johnnie'. By this he meant that the firm imported machines and he put them into running order, whereupon they were sold at a profit. 'If I wanted to work in a shop.' he said, 'I wouldn't have trained as an engineer,' so when he was offered a post as Chief Engineer on a sugar plantation, we moved from the city to the country.

There were two females of importance on this plantation. The human one was the owner, an elderly lady whom I have com-memorated as Madame Dulac and the machine one was a size-able sugar factory and rum distillery, stuffed to the roofs with machines. Our employer was a Scotswoman, benevolent in a feudal way, who took an interest in all the doings in the develop-ing island where the ox-drawn cart was just giving way to the truck and the agricultural tractor, where people were importing and trying to use machinery of which they had little or no understanding. When machinery owned by her acquaintances went wrong, our employer would say: 'I'll send my Scottish engineer over,' so that Sandy found himself from time to time in very odd places indeed, such as sauce and toffee factories, and examining pumps at the bottom of wells.

An enterprising Chinese imported an entire automatic bakery and was soon supplying bread to half the island and all went merrily until the evening of the last day of one year when something went wrong and the bakery 'shut down'. Things did not break down or go wrong in the island, they did not become inoperative, they 'shut down'. The cook would forget to put paraffin in the cooker and it would shut down and the yard boy would accidentally drop his cutlass through the garden hose and it would shut down. So the bakery shut down and our employer said she would send her Scottish engineer over and I said, 'On Hogmanay? Well, I am coming with you.' (I have told you of my primitive religion and I was determined to be with Sandy for the coming of the New Year.)

After driving some fifty miles through the tropical dark, we arrived at the bakery to find the big building ablaze with lights inside and out and the owner and the entire staff standing outside the closed doors.

'What's up?' Sandy asked.

'It shut down, sah.'

Sandy pulled open one half of the big sliding doors, whereupon a large lump of dough came flying out and stuck to the windscreen of the car. Inside the building, there was a barrage of lumps of dough flying in all directions and other lumps stuck on walls, ceiling, windows, floor.

'Where's your main switch?' Sandy yelled and the owner pointed to a door in the far corner of the inside of the building and I watched Sandy run towards the door, dodging like a Rugby player not carrying a ball but trying to evade the flying balls of dough.

When the first machine in the production line had gone out of kilter, the Chinese owner and his staff had simply made a run for it. It had never occurred to them to throw the main switch and cut off all activity, so that a chain reaction had been set up, culminating in a sinister uncanny machine called a 'Former and Hander-up' which had arms, hands and fingers that shaped the dough and slid the loaves on to a conveyor belt. It was a lurid nightmarish scene, which I shall never forget, of machinery on the rampage with about thirty men totally at its mercy.

And now I come back to my hen, Chickabird. About three times each year, she would very cunningly lay a clutch of eggs in some hidden place on the moor or about the steading and in due course would arrive in the yard at hen-feeding time with about a dozen little chicks. She was a devoted mother and would tackle any enemy in defence of her brood, but a day would come when she would decide that they must fend for themselves and if they clustered around her, expecting her to scratch for them, she would peck them quite viciously and chase them away. I think, perhaps, that I write novels as Chickabird hatched chicks and how other, when you think of it, would a Highland crofter like me write novels? And when a novel has reached the stage of being out in the world and able to fend for itself, I no longer want to be bothered with it. I want, like Chickabird, to set about hiding the next lot of eggs and hatching out the next brood.

Probably this is why I do not go about my work in a business-like way, working regular hours and keeping diaries and note-books. If one writes because of some compulsive instinct, one does not need and indeed one has not the time to keep diaries and notebooks. One does the weekly wash, carries in the firewood and having ignored the interior pressure for as long as possible, the moment comes when one simply has to sit down and write. One faces the fact that the steam is building to pressure-point and that God is not going to pick up the pen.

Chapter 10

Why did you begin to write the JEAN ROBERTSON *series when the* REACHFAR *series was so popular and so much nicer?*
Because I was tired of being totally identified with Janet Reachfar.

Another of my defects as a writer is that I can write only in the first person. I have to think myself into the character of the narrator and go on from there. I have written only one thing in the third person which is the short text of a picture book for children and I found the method extremely artificial but I was assured that an 'I' book for children was 'completely out' and allowed myself to be talked into the project. When I was a young child, however, reading the *Jolly Books* and the Blackie's *Children's Annuals* which were given to me at Christmas, I can remember the nag at the back of my mind : 'Who *is* this person who is telling me this story about Betty and the cherry tree? Is it her mother or her Uncle George?' However, all sorts of conventions and rigidities build up in the writing world as in every other world and although publishers are reputed to be seeking, always, for an 'original voice', it often seems that any deviation from the norm is suspect.

Having 'got away with' the 'unusual' *My Friend Muriel* in the first person and having continued with the Reachfar series, some of the letters I received made me feel that George's pronouncement that I was the biggest liar in the country was true, for people began to send messages of goodwill to some of my characters who did not exist except in fiction but the very words 'fiction' and 'novels' had gone out of the window. People had decided that the Reachfar series was straight autobiography, Janet Reachfar and I were one person and tourists began to ask people on the roads of the Black Isle the way to Reachfar.

In my usual ill-natured way, I complained to my editor about this in the course of one of my visits to London, in the words : 'It makes me feel that I can't write at all, only tell people about my operation like that woman I met in the train,' and he in his customary constructive way replied: 'Then write a novel that is nothing to do with Reachfar and if you make a go of it, we'll publish it.' He also told me, by the way, that I should be pleased rather than annoyed that readers thought Janet was a real person and Reachfar a real place but I am never pleased with anything connected with my writing. What I write invariably causes me some sort of dissatisfaction.

Nothing came of his suggestion about a novel unconnected with Reachfar for a long time, but around 1967 I came to the discovery that from the time of my birth until I was twenty-one, my life had revolved round two poles, two places radically different from one another, Dunbartonshire and Glasgow, my 'away home' being one and The Colony, my 'real home', being the other. I had confined my writing to the idyllic pole of The Colony, where life was good, easy and free under a wide sky and had ignored the harsh pole of all the slums I had seen and known, where life was cruel, bestial and constricted but still managed to survive.

I have told you where and how I saw my first submarine and life being made up of the rough as well as the smooth, I will now tell you where and how I saw my first louse. It was on my fourth birthday, the tenth of March, 1914. It was a cold wet day in the Vale of Leven, a place that is, or was then, less beautiful than its name and my birthday dumpling had just been put on the fire to boil. We would have it for supper when my father came off duty at five-thirty. My mother was knitting, for my sister Catherine was to be born a month later and I was reading a picture book when my father's voice came unexpectedly and long before five-thirty from the office passage. We lived in a little ground-floor flat in this police station, two other policemen and their families lived in the flats above and the flats were connected to the offices and cells by a staircase and the office passage.

'Jessie!' he called. My mother's name was Janet but he called her Jessie. 'Light the boiler!'

This was all most extraordinary. My mother went out to the passage, came back, opened a drawer and took out a big double sheet. Then she went out again and brought my father in with the sheet covering him from top to toe. He was walking inside it as if he were in a sack. He was a big man who looked bigger still inside the sheet and he told me everything was all right and not to be afraid as he walked past me, walking as if he did not want to touch anything or even have the sheet that was under his feet touch the floor.

He went into the wash-house off the scullery where there was a sink and a cement floor and here my mother took the corners of the sheet from his shoulders and spread it all over the floor around him, exposing his dripping wet, navy-blue rain-cape. Rooted to the spot in the doorway which my mother had told me not to pass, I saw not one louse but thousands, crawling over the blue cape, the trousers, even over the black boots. But this was not the worst. He loosened the neck-clasp, let the cape drop down on to the sheet and my mother said: 'Oh, my God, Duncan!' I had never heard her say such a thing before and had never heard such horror in her voice. He was holding in his arms a naked baby whose skin was almost covered with the brown scabs of some form of eczema and among the raised edges of the scabs, the lice crawled in and out like grey troglodytes in a rocky landscape of solidified brown lava.

I remember little more except the boiler fire making a red blaze, my mother sponging the thin little body with swabs of cotton wool over the luke-warm water in the sink and the strong smell of Jeyes' Fluid that came from my father's bath. The amazing thing is that that under-nourished, neglected, eczema and louse-ridden baby lived and so too did his three sisters and four brothers who, my father said later, had been in an even filthier condition than the baby. The Salvation Army had taken charge of the older seven while my father brought the baby to my mother and his colleagues took the fighting-drunk parents into the cells. A doctor and two women came and took the baby away, wearing a napkin out of Catherine's stock and wrapped in a piece of blanket. Then we had my fourth birthday supper. I remember my mother's eyes looking surreptitiously behind my father's ears as she poured tea.

At this stage, the origins of the names I use in my writing may be becoming obvious. My mother's maiden name was Janet Sandison, my father was Duncan Cameron and I was baptised Elizabeth Jane. I took my mother's name for my heroine of the Reachfar series and my own second name added to my father's forename for my pseudonym, by way of a belated tribute to my dead parents.

So in this year of 1967, when I remembered this other pole of my life, I remembered also what my editor had said and I remembered too that in a novel of the Reachfar series, *My Friends the Macleans*, recently written, I had given to Janet Sandison, my heroine, my own vice of writing in secret. Why not write Janet's novel for her and send it to my editor by way of a joke? The joke, sarcastically entitled *The Glory of the Spring* at that time, was mailed in a large chocolate box with a spray of pink roses on its lid in November of 1968 and was subsequently re-titled *Jean in the Morning*.

In spite of George's pronouncement that I am the biggest liar in the country, I try not to 'lie' in my writing and I do not merely 'imagine' either. I fictionalise my own experience and when I began to write about Jean Robertson and the slums, I was in some difficulty, for I had no personal experience of the squalor and filth of a slum home. I had, however, seen some humble homes kept by women who were so fanatically 'clean' that the very air around them was sterile and it was out of those that Jean's mother and her economy were born. Jean's outdoor life in the backyards and gutters was as I had observed the life of children in and around Glasgow, including the drunk men being thrown out of the pubs while the band of the Salvation Army played 'Shall we gather at the River?' And ever since I was old enough to understand their ugly trade, I had hated the pawnshops where women lost for ever their dearest possessions for a few pence to feed their children, while my father and his colleagues brought their husbands into the cells with the week's pay in the form of whisky in their bellies.

When Catherine was one month old, in May of 1914, we moved to a station at Balloch at the foot of Loch Lomond, then there was the holiday at The Colony when George and I put Angus down the stable drain and the next event of that year that I remember was the earth-shaking outbreak of the Great War on the fourth of August.

Shortly after that, Balloch Castle and estate were sold and turned into a furlough home for colonial troops on leave from France and now the gay ladies with the frilly petticoats moved into various houses in Balloch, causing the respectable citizenry, of course, to complain to the police.

The concept of the golden-hearted tart is said to be a cliché but it is like the artist starving in his garret and has a grain of truth behind it. The leading personality of the gay invaders of Balloch was known to my father and his colleagues as 'the Black Diamond' and when not otherwise engaged, she would walk about the little town with a group of her friends, talking to everybody, throwing insults at those who did not respond to her friendly overtures, giving sweets and pennies to the children but not to me. She knew that I was the policeman's child but bore me no ill-will for that. If we encountered one another, she would look down at me, her dark eyes brilliant under her raven hair, laugh and say pleasantly in her broad Glasgow accent: 'Tell that big braw daddy o' yours that the Black Diamon' is behaving hersel', will ye, hen?' Then she would laugh and go on her way.

When Balloch Castle was sold, the sale of the indoor effects comprised many articles of value and my father was posted on duty among this display. In recompense for this extra duty, the owners gave him two articles which I still have in the house here, the small mahogany box with the brass lock and a slit in the lid which sat on a table in the hall of the castle and into which the household put their letters for the post and a small oak chest of drawers from one of the servants' bedrooms which, people tell me, has a value now that it did not have then. I mention these things because they cannot speak for themselves to record their own history.

The Up-the-Burn escapades of Jean Robertson's life were born out of memories of a later date and another place. On the outskirts of this small town, there was another wealthy estate with a very ill-tempered head gamekeeper who was always laying complaints with my father about the local children raiding the woods for conkers and fishing for minnows in the stream. His name, I now remember, was Willie Robertson and he was a bachelor who lived alone except for four savage retriever dogs. In order to pacify him, my father used to invite him to supper with us sometimes and I remember a supper of boiled ham and salad when Willie stuffed too large a piece of ham into his mouth, did not masticate it thoroughly enough, choked and went purple in the face. My father removed the piece of ham from his throat with a pair of pliers.

'Ill-natured old devil,' he said when Willie had gone home. 'I should have let him choke. What harm are the bairns doing up there? They only need to feel the grass under their feet,' and then to me: 'But don't *you* go over that estate wall, mind.' The policeman's child had to be beyond reproach but, fortunately, my need to feel the grass under my feet was less acute than that of the other children of the district. I had the grass and heather of The Colony under my feet for two months in the summer and for shorter periods at Christmas and Easter.

Many snippets of varied experience come together to form the fabric of a novel but I think that this fabric is stretched like the canvas of a tent over the supports of a few basic, deeply-felt beliefs. I have, for as long as I can remember, disliked and distrusted the idea of accumulated wealth and this is one of the supporting struts of the Jean Robertson novels. I think this dislike and distrust were engendered in the first place, like so many of my beliefs, by George, that cuckoo in the nest of the Cameron family.

My grandparents, my parents, all the members of my family were thrifty and it was regarded as a virtue to save money and put it in the bank while to 'lift' capital from the bank for any purpose, other than a great emergency like a funeral, was regarded as a vice. George, however, was different from the rest. That clown, my grandmother would have told you, was not to be trusted with money at all, so little so that my grandfather, on receiving a pound or two for a pig, locked it in the 'kist' in his bedroom and it remained there, along with any other sums received in the course of the year until my father came home on leave and was entrusted to take the cache to the bank in Cromarty.

I do not know factually how this distrust of George arose but can imagine that, long before I was born, he had received the money for a bullock at the auction mart in Dingwall and had used it either to go on a spree with his cronies or to give away to someone whose need he judged to be greater than that of the Camerons. What is fact, however, is that when my grandfather went upstairs to put a sum in the kist, George would say to me: 'There's Granda off up to say his prayers,' whereupon my grandmother would snap: 'That's enough! Are you two going to lead in that hay today or just sit about the house on your behinds?' George and I would go out, yoke the horses and go down to the hayfield but, once there, it was ten-to-one that he would say something like: 'Ach, to the devil with it! I am not in the mood for the hay. Just you tie the horses to the east fence out of sight of the house and we'll go down the burn and see can we guddle a trout or two.' George did not believe in the hymn that exhorted him to work for the night is coming. George worked according to his mood but he was always in the mood for something and when my grandmother took the trout from us to fry them for supper, she would remark that we had not led much hay home that afternoon but that the trout were real bonnie.

George, in the mood to hoe turnips, could hoe twice as fast as any other man in the district, leaving behind him a row of evenly-spaced little plants sitting on a ridge as clean-cut as a well-pitched roof. In the mood to cut roads round the edges of a field of oats with a scythe, the road that the horses and reaper would use, he could swing along rhythmically behind the long flashing blade at twice the speed of any other man. And he worked with magnificent ease, tall, spare and straight. No matter how hot the day, George never took off his old tweed coat, never rolled up his sleeves and never shed a drop of sweat. He never gave the impression of bending his back. He moved behind the plough and pair of horses with his back as straight as a Seaforth Highlander on the march. And he was never flustered, always had time to leave what he was doing and come with me up to the moor to be told that this little flower that caught flies in its leaves that were like little hands was called Sundew. And on Fridays, when we went to Cromarty and I had a ha'penny to buy toffee, he would throw another ha'penny on the counter and say to the sweetie-wife: 'To the devil with poverty, Maggie. Give her a big bar.'

The extraordinary thing that my grandparents and my father could explain only as God moving in a mysterious way was that, in spite of all their thrift and saving, George always outstripped them in wealth and I do not mean metaphorical wealth but actual hard cash in the bank. It happened in this way. My grandfather's sister Bella had been in the service, nearly all her life, of a wealthy old bachelor, ending up as his housekeeper and when he died, he left her a fair amount of money.

She was a very secretive old lady who proceeded to live out her life in a single room in Cromarty. She had little use for any of us but when George was in the mood, he would cut and cart down to her a load of firewood or catch a pair of rabbits for her or take to her, without my grandmother knowing, a clutch of eggs from the nest of some hen that was 'laying away'. My Chickabird had tacit permission to lay away because she was so good at rearing her chickens but the other hens were very carefully watched, only George was even cleverer than my grandmother at knowing which hens were indulging in this lawless activity. George, like the rest of us, thought that Great-aunt Bella was really poor and she gave him little thanks for his attentions during her lifetime but when she died she left him all she had.

Then there was Great-grand-uncle Kenneth, an uncle of my grandmother who lived to a tremendous and eccentric age, part of the time with one of my aunts, part of the time at The Colony, after his retirement, this was. At the age of fifteen, Uncle Kenneth had gone to New Zealand in a sailing ship in which there was, among the other passengers, an Irishman who was told by a member of the crew that there were kangaroos in New Zealand as big as houses and very savage. This was a wicked lie, Uncle Kenneth said and the sailor should never have said such a thing for it so terrified the Irishman that he jumped overboard in the Timor Sea with the intention of swimming back to Ireland. The crew only got him back inboard before the sharks got him, Uncle Kenneth said.

The world seems smaller and less wonderful now than it seemed when Uncle Kenneth told me stories of New Zealand and the people nowadays seem to be less picturesque. There is a lady in this district who thinks nothing of flying off to New Zealand each year to visit her married daughter and her grandchildren and the rest of us think nothing of her flights either. Do you notice the phrase 'think nothing'? It seems to me sad that one result of advanced technology is to make us think nothing of a journey to the other side of the earth. That he had been to New Zealand gave Uncle Kenneth an aura of the picturesque and adventurous and it was exciting to look at George and think to yourself that he had seen the Sphinx and the Khyber Pass.

My childhood was long past before I discovered that a man once lived in this district who was the hero of a heroic episode, a man picturesque in more ways than one. My editor, in 1964, presented me with a book entitled *The Day of Reckoning* by Mary Clive. It is a charming book, in which the writer 'resuscitates some of the commonplaces of my childhood', a childhood of the early years of the present century. The book contains many pictures of many facets of life at the time with which it deals, including reproductions of the pictures which hung on the walls of the rooms which the writer remembers. The title of the book, *The Day of Reckoning*, was also the title of one of those remembered pictures, a typical Victorian moral-pointing work.

George spent an evening with the book and at bedtime, when I had stopped writing, he asked: 'Are all the pictures in this book kind of famous? It says that a lot of them are in art galleries.'

'Yes. A lot of them are quite well known.'

'The Tate Gallery is very famous, isn't it?'

'Yes. Why?'

'There is a picture of Doctor Brydon in it, it says here. I wonder if he ever knew?'

I felt a little lost. 'Doctor Brydon? What picture?'

George handed me the book open at the page with the reproduction of 'The Remnants of an Army' by Lady Butler, the picture of a severely-wounded man being carried by, as opposed to riding, an exhausted-looking horse. The caption under the picture said it was executed in 1879, the year of George's birth and then went on: 'The end of the British retreat from Cabul in 1842. "One man alone reached Jellalabad to tell the tale. Literally one man, Doctor Brydon, came to Jellalabad out of a moving host which had numbered in all some sixteen thousand when it set out on its march." – Justin McCarthy. *History of Our Own Times*.'

'He never mentioned the picture,' George said when I looked up.

'Are you telling me that you knew this Doctor Brydon?' I asked.

'Surely. He used to live in that big house next to the manse on this side of Cromarty.'

'You knew him to speak to?'

'Am I not telling you? He was very delicate in his stomach as an old man.' Looking at the picture, I found this easy to believe. 'I was never very fond of going to school, as you know and on my way I was always very glad to see Miss Brydon waiting at the end of their avenue. She would be needing me to go and find peewits' eggs for the Doctor. Your father used to argue that school was more important but I always went after the Doctor's eggs. He used to tell grand yarns about India, about Kabul and the great march from Kabul to Kandahar but he never mentioned about his picture being painted.'

The weather of the world. That day when George went to the circus and joined the Seaforth Highlanders, were the grand yarns told by Doctor Brydon about India in the depths of his mind? But back to Uncle Kenneth.

Sharks or not, he reached New Zealand, cleared some land and prospered, cleared more land and prospered some more and finished up with quite a large sheep farm. In about 1920 he sold this and retired home to the Highlands where he farmed for a time, then retired finally but lived on for years after that. He grew very deaf, was very fierce, with a pointed grey beard and a hooked nose and George was the only one of the family who could make him hear, not by shouting at him as the rest of us did but by some trick of timbre that got through to his shut-in world. Then Uncle Kenneth died, leaving the remains of his fortune to George who promptly gave half to me and half to my brother. This was in 1939. My father was horrified.

'Jock is only nineteen,' he protested, 'and you know how reckless Bet is although she is twenty-nine. She has never saved a penny all the years she has been working. They will only *spend* it!'

'And that's more than I'll do, here on The Colony hill,' said George.

In that period after I left the university and before I went to work, I was at The Colony for the best part of a year and I remember when George and I began to cart the dung out from the midden to spread it on the fields before he began to plough. 'Be canny with the dung,' my grandmother told us. 'It has to go a long way,' but down on the field George said: 'Dump it on thick, Bet. This is the tattie field. If you don't put anything in, you won't get anything out. Himself can dig into the kist and buy some fertiliser if we run short.'

George was a putter-in, in the way of firewood for a cranky old woman, and voice timbre for a deaf old man and I think it good that justice was done in the end and George got something out. And it also had its comic side which he did not miss.

'Do you think I should get a kist?' he asked me in the stable while the rest of the family, in the house, were trying to get over the contents of Great-aunt Bella's will, 'and be upsides with Granda?' and then, the laughter gone from his voice: 'All that money in the world, lying in kists and banks. It's a wonder it doesn't go rotten.'

My grandmother used to be critical of the time I 'wasted', in finding out the names of wild flowers, the different names for different formations of cloud and so on and once, when I was quite young, when she caught me reciting part of the 'Lay of the Last Minstrel' to George at his request—

The way was long, the wind was cold,
The minstrel was infirm and old—

when we should have been doing something 'useful', she said: 'A lot of good this idling will do *you* two when you are infirm and old.'

'She means,' George explained when she had gone, 'that we should be working to have money in the bank when we are infirm and old. Never heed her.' Then came the chuckling laugh: 'Your head is as full of words as a bank is of money. I wonder if words make interest like money?' We had a good laugh at this idea which would have shocked my grandmother so much and then: 'Well, go on and tell me a bittie more about this poor old minstrel craitur.'

Down the years, I listened to George and in 1967 his attitude to wealth, coloured further by my own mind, began to come out on to paper in words on which interest had accrued as one of the tent supports of the Jean Robertson tetralogy. Much of what I am and believe came from George but my grandparents and my parents and the maternal grandparents who died before I was born were all 'in it', I suppose, as Jean Robertson would put it.

My father, the policeman temporarily, but the eternal crofter, was much more a man of the land than George was. George was a skilled worker of the land but I do not think he had the deep, heart-blood tie with the land that my father had.

My father, for most of the time, was a strictly conventional man, a kindly public-spirited man, the chairman in his retirement of the local social committee and of course a strict upholder of the law which he had served for thirty-two years, the sort of man deeply respected in a country community. When The Colony was sold and George joined my father and Kirsty at the cottage in Jemimaville, an explosive element entered the house. The brothers were devoted to one another but George had no respect for anybody in particular although respecting everybody in a deep and true way and did not value respect

115

for himself as my father did. George saw that kind of respect as a barrier between people.

At this time, my brother was master of a little country school about fifteen miles from here and my niece Shona had just been born, my father's first grandchild and of tremendous pride to him and both his own village and my brother's village pleased him greatly with their congratulations. Then, one day, a disturbing story reached my father's ears. George had wheeled Shona, about two months old, along my brother's village in her pram, to the push-bar of which a bicycle bell had been attached and he tinkled the bell all the way along to the pub. At the pub, the bell gave a long peal, the publican was seen to come out with half-a-dozen large bottles of beer and place them in the pram at the baby's feet, whereupon George and Shona made their tinkling way back to the schoolhouse. (This episode, by the way – I was in the West Indies when it took place – was told to me not by my father or George but by my brother, with great glee.)

My father, wearing his policeman's face, had George on the carpet. There were only eighteen months of age between them but my father gave the impression of being a wise, experienced, responsible man, which he was, while George always had the air of a mischievous schoolboy. At this time, they were straddling man's allotted lifespan of seventy.

'Did you fix that bell to the baby's pram?' my father asked.

'Surely.'

'And take her along to the pub, ringing that bell for the whole village to hear?'

'Yes. I always buy some beer for Jock's house when I go along to see them. Your grand-daughter may be the finest baby in the country but she is too young yet to go into pubs.'

George had decided that grandfather's pride was verging on the pompous and pricked the balloon with the tinkle of a bicycle bell and there came a time when I felt I was being blown up into a romantic balloon by the Reachfar novels and I endeavoured to prick that balloon with Jean Robertson.

I notice that once or twice in these chapters I have referred to my father's 'policeman's face' and this family expression was originated by myself when I was very young. I do not remember much about the incident but I remember the shocking moment of discovery that a well-known, much-loved person, in a different situation from the usual, can become alarmingly different and totally unknown. The occasion was a Royal Progress through the towns of Clydeside and the Vale of Leven – the personages would have been King George V and Queen Mary – and policemen's wives had the small privilege of places at the edges of the crowded pavements. I was in a push-chair or go-cart as they were called in those days. It had a seat and back-rest made of red carpet, I remember.

I do not remember the preliminaries but I remember the noise of the brass band as the cavalcade approached down the cleared street and right in front was *my father*, riding a big grey horse. My mother, like everybody else in those patriotic days of 1912 or 1913, would have been watching the approach of the royal carriage and I got away, out of the push-chair into the middle of the street, my arms upheld as I shouted, 'Daddy! Daddy!' expecting to be taken up to ride in front of him as I did at The Colony with him and George. And then I saw the stern face I had never seen before as he looked down at me and said: 'You bad girl! Go back to Mother!'

Completely overcome, I sat down on the cold, wet granite setts of the street – I can still feel their chill in my behind – and yelled my outrage, outdoing the brass band until my affronted mother grabbed me and scuttled back to the pavement. When I recovered sufficiently to speak, I have been told, all I would say was: 'That policeman's face! That policeman's face!' Until the day my father died, the policeman's face was something to be reckoned with but we of the family did not see it very often.

There is another little tale of that Royal Progress which I heard much later, which now comes back to me and which I shall tell because I like the poetic justice of its ending. I think I can truthfully say that none of us Camerons have been thrusters, pushers-forward or in any way aggressive or ambitious. We are the sort who are left on the platform or at the bus-stop in the rush-hour.

In those years before the First World War, Dunbartonshire had no mounted police force and for occasions such as the Royal Progress, horses were hired from livery stables and policemen who could ride rode them. Many policemen could ride or at least sit on a horse, for many of them were Highlanders like my father who had been brought up on the land and they would go to the livery stables some days before to make the acquaintance of their mounts. Characteristically, with less cunning than his fellows, my father was the last man, at the time of this Progress, to go to the livery stable and when he got there he found that the only horse left for him was what he described at first sight as 'this dirty, ill-natured, big grey brute with one silver eye'. He had a terrible time with the animal on the way to the railway station where the procession was to form. Much to the amusement of his colleagues, it bucked, reared and tried every trick to unseat him and he arrived at the station still on board but extremely anxious about the long, slow parade that was to come. Then the steam train came whistling into the station, the brass band began to play and the big grey brute, which was an old cavalry horse, stood to attention with his ears cocked while all the others began to rear and threw half of their not very expert riders. This was how my father came to be leading the diminished remnants of an army, the Mounted Police Guard, which I did my best to bring to a halt.

In the course of the last few paragraphs I may seem to have digressed a long way from the question as to why I began to write the Jean Robertson tetralogy, but have I? Think of the ambitions of Jean's mother and their sorry ending and think of Jean's lack of ambition and the contentment she found in her unaggressive little life. The influences of my family seem to permeate all my ideas and show through everything I write, especially the ideas of George.

George had a strong dislike of class distinctions and few of the land-owners in this district in his childhood were as kindly as Doctor Brydon, who took a barefoot crofter boy into his study and told him tales of India. And like Ernest Hemingway, my typewriter and my brother Jock, George had a built-in, shock-proof **** detector.

During the 1914–1918 war, the high life of the 'big houses' was still a feature of this area, with house parties, shooting parties and dinner parties, for the Fleet was lying in the Firth with officers to be entertained anent the marrying off of daughters and one of the favourite pastimes of the more mature ladies visiting the big houses was painting pictures of my grandfather, seated on a bench at the end of the house, his walking stick beside him, his collie dog at his feet, his waist-long white beard blowing in the breeze under his eagle's beak of a nose, the proud old clansman of cloud-cuckoo romance to the last whisker. He was born in 1838 so, in 1917, he would be seventy-nine. The ladies and many of the people round about thought their pictures were ever so nice and *just* like old Cameron-The-Colony but George had another view. 'They should paint him counting the money in his kist,' he said to me one day when we were stacking the hay.

I never really came to know my grandfather although he lived to the age of ninety-six. The difference in our ages was so great, he being seventy-nine when I was seven while, also, he was a very silent man who seldom spoke to any of us except my grandmother and my father. My father took the conventional attitude that the grandparents were to be respected whatever their characters and he venerated his father while George liked better my grandmother and she, in spite of calling him a clown and scolding him constantly, secretly regarded him as her favourite child of the five who remained alive.

My father started his police service in 1899 at the age of twenty-one in the then little town of Helensburgh on the estuary of the Clyde. It was a wealthy place at the time, with the houses of the working-class huddled by the water and the 'big houses' of the wealthy on the hill behind. The young policemen were given most of the night duty and there was much larking about between nine and midnight between them and the servant girls among the rhododendrons of the gardens that surrounded the big villas. But my father did not meet my mother among the rhododendrons. She was lady's-maid-companion to a rich old spinster who drove about on fine days in an open landau, accompanied by my mother, and my father, when on daytime points duty, would hold up the landau, to the fury of the coachman, while he ogled my mother. From this it was only a step to the back door of the villa, the housekeeper's and butler's room and then the official walking-out. I do not know when the holding up of the landau began or how long was the walking-out, but they were married in 1909.

Like all of us, my parents used often to talk of the happy days of the past and in the dark winter evenings, before my bedtime, while I sat between them with my book on my lap, I heard much of the goings-on in these wealthy houses on the Helensburgh hills. As a married man, my father had been moved to his new station in the Vale of Leven and now perhaps the talk of Helensburgh was an escape from the drunkenness and the neglected children.

There was a period, often recalled, when the foregathering of the young policemen and the servant girls on the dark evenings was legitimised temporarily because a ghost was haunting the dark road up from the town to the villas. The servant girls, some of whom had been terrified by the ghost, had to be escorted home after their few hours of free time. It was some months before the ghost was finally laid and discovered to be an ingenious arrangement of white sheet, ropes and wires, operated from behind a high wall by a schoolboy in his teens. The boy, John Logie Baird, grew up to invent television. It is of interest, I think, that one of his earlier inventions should have been a ghost, preceding the bigger, better, more intrusive ghost of television.

Another story I heard of the houses on the hill was of the three maiden sisters who lived in poverty in one room of an enormous house with one very old servant and when the last of them died, a distant relative inherited hundreds of thousands of pounds as well as the house, its contents and all the gold sovereigns hidden under carpets, in vases and under their mattresses.

What you learn young, as my grandmother said, you never forget and it seems that the Jean Robertson sequence has been growing in my mind since before I first read of Alphonse Daudet's rabbits. I was twelve then, but my mother died when I was ten and after her death I heard no more of the courtship days among the big houses on the hill.

Chapter 11

You have said you have no children. How did you come to write your books for young people and My Friends the Hungry Generation?
Because I like children.

When Sandy and I came on leave to this country in 1956, we stayed with my brother and sister-in-law and met my nephews Neil and Donald, the new baby, for the first time. My niece, Shona, we had met some years earlier as a toddler. When I came home to this village for good in 1959, my new nephew, the little Mongol, Iain was not quite one year old but Donald was now nearly four and like his older brother and sister had developed a distinct personality of his own. I was fascinated by the resemblances and the differences between all four children and a little envious of my brother and sister-in-law in having achieved this brood.

I arrived at the cottage in January and Jock, Betty and the four children arrived for the Easter holidays so that there were eight, with the inclusion of George and myself, in the little house and it seemed to be about to disintegrate with the exuberance of the children. The three older ones seemed to be constantly in a state of crisis, in fits of laughter or floods of tears, quarrelling and composing their differences. They shouted and banged doors, ate themselves into a state of stupefaction, fought about who was to help bath the baby and cheated one another mercilessly at card games like rummy. Gone were the restrictions of my own upbringing. This lot were being allowed to be people, but fairly civilised people. Jock's blue eyes could take on a certain look that could stop a fight before it could start. I was so bemused by the noise, so worried by the savagery of their quarrels, so incredulous at their ingenuity as card-cheats that the ten-day stay was a most traumatic experience but I think that visit was the genesis of *My Friends the Hungry Generation*.

What perplexed me entirely was my brother's unruffled un-
worried calm in the midst of it all. With sheer mayhem going
on around him while they enacted the misdeeds of Para Handy
in the tiny sitting-room, he would sit doing the current Penguin
Book of crossword puzzles but then he was a schoolmaster and
I had seen him several times with his some hundred pupils
gathered round him in the playground like a brood of chickens,
all talking at once. He is tall like the rest of the family and
standing or sitting still in the midst of a group of romping
children, he has a monolithic look which perhaps gives them a
feeling of security and makes them like him as much as they
do.

It will be obvious from the fact that my first novel was not
published until I was forty-nine years old that I am a slow developer but Jock is the reverse. Of course, he had the advantage
of the daily company of George from infancy until he went to
university and had not my disadvantage of being called a fool by
Kirsty with monotonous frequency throughout his adolescence,
but these are merely excuses for myself that I am making. Jock
is the family brain and I might as well admit it and be done
with it. His pose as the Scottish country dominie does not conceal, except from a fool, what he is. And nothing can conceal
his passion for children, especially children who have difficulty
in learning at school. He can battle for hours, days, weeks,
months against some obscure psychological block that prevents
a child from learning to read and has never had a failure. 'It
must be a question of understanding,' he says, 'and if you keep
at it long enough, you find the breakthrough in the end.'

Despite the ten years of difference in our ages, he and I were
always very close and my holiday arrivals at The Colony
throughout the 1920s were always a deep joy to both of us. We
had little contact with one another during the 1930s when I was
in London and he was at his academy and then at university
but, in 1939, when the war began, he joined the Navy and I
joined the Women's Auxiliary Air Force and because of the
feeling of upheaval and the disintegration of the life we had
known, I suppose, we began to write to one another. I wish now
that these letters had been preserved, especially those written
by Jock but war is a time of being prepared, always, to move
quickly and travel light.

Because of the censorship of mail, we could not write about

*Seaforth Highlander
George Cameron, aged
twenty-one (right)*

*George at Jemimaville,
aged eighty-two*

*Sandy in
uniform, 1943*

*'The Hungry Generation' – Neil, Shona, Donald
and baby Iain*

our daily lives and work, so we wrote about George's 'yarns', recalling them for one another and about the various neighbours who lived around The Colony. In this way, we got ourselves into more trouble with the censorship than if he had written me the disposition of the entire British Fleet and if I had written him a report of current Air Force strategy.

This district, in earlier times, was much given to the endowing of people with bye- or nick-names and there was an old crofter who used to call his large scattered family in from the fields and sheep-runs by blowing a whistle. This earned him the bye-name of 'Toot'. Sandy Toot grew old and died in the fulness of time but the bye-name descended to his progeny, one of whom was a daughter of the generation of George, who was known as Belle Toot. I had been home here on leave and on my return to my unit, I wrote to Jock that I had seen Belle Toot 'sailing past with a fairish list to starboard' but, probably because I had been working with aerial photographs of France that day, I spelled the name 'Belle Toute'. Jock was had on the mat by the officer in charge of mail in his ship and severely questioned about this report on '– *Belle Toute*. Was she a French trawler?'

Then Jock came home here on leave and wrote to me: 'The Arran Chiefs and Arran Banners are heaving over the sky-line,' and it was my turn for the mat at my unit. Were these code names and if so, for what? I had quite a time of it convincing the censor that they were code names for potato plants heaving against the skyline of The Colony hill. Jock and I would have been conspicuously unsuccessful as members of a Fifth Column.

Jock knew of my anxiety about him and always found some way, in his letters, of making sure that I knew he was safely ashore for a short spell and I have always remembered the letter which informed me: 'I am a member of a gardening squad at the moment and I have a lovely watering-can on wheels which I port at the short trail.'

We both have a tendency to claustrophobia, perhaps because our spiritual home is The Colony, under its wide dome of sky and Jock, although he never spoke of it if he could help it, must have suffered terribly as an Asdic operator in a blister on the keel of the aircraft-carrier HMS *Indefatigable*. For many years after he left the Navy, he could not enter a concert hall, a cinema or any crowded place and when people said how fortunate he had been to come through the six years 'without a scratch', I knew there were more than scratches under the surface.

During the war, he and I spent a short leave together at The Colony with George, our father spending one day in our company before giving up and remaining at home in the village. Jock and I tarred the corrugated iron roofs of the house and steading, he wearing dungarees and I wearing what had been a white aertex shirt and dungarees. We had a rope tied round the chimney of the house with a basket on its end in which, when required, George sent up bottles of beer. My father maintained until he died that we did not wash even our faces for ten days. And while we tarred and drank beer, we talked incessantly about everything under the sun, emphasising our points with our tar brushes.

Jock was as good as Ernest Hemingway or my typewriter at the detection of shit and I particularly remember that, as I sat astride the roof-ridge, I began to rave somewhat excessively about a film performance by the actor, Charles Boyer. Jock heard me out, then looking to the far summit of Ben Wyvis, said quietly: 'It is a pity that he is such a wee mannie. When he goes to kiss the heroine, I've heard, they have to dig a hole for her to stand in.' The solid rock of hard sense crops out through Jock's character as the whinstone boulders crop out among the heather of The Colony moor.

Jock is the only person other than George and Sandy with whom I have ever been able to talk quite without reserve (I speak of the time before I began to write this letter!) and if I was shy and reticent, Jock was notoriously so at that time but he talked to me and, of course, to Betty who had been his sweetheart since they first met at Aberdeen University. When the war ended, they were married, then Sandy and I went to the West Indies and Jock and I wrote to one another now only at times of crisis, such as the death of our father, but the bond between us held, the close intimacy was always there, an intimacy that does not need words or only words obscure to other people such as Jock's remark on my going to the West Indies with Sandy: 'Well, at long last somebody is taking a notion and going down to Wick!'

You may have noticed that, above, I said that Jock, George and Sandy were the only people with whom I could talk without reserve, but as soon as these words were on paper, I saw that they were not precisely true. I had never told any of those three most intimate people of my desire to write. Other than the woman who told me not to be stupid, the only person I had ever told of this desire was my father and this was in the miserable days of the Trade Depression when, in a fit of near-despair, I told him that I did not care by what means I earned my living because the only thing I wanted to do was to write. Perhaps it was his look of startled wonder dying away into his belief that young people outgrow their dreams that was the beginning of my secrecy but he remembered what I had said because, before he died, he told Jock of this early ambition of mine so that, when I wrote from the West Indies that I had had three novels accepted and was coming home, Jock replied: 'I am glad that this old dream of yours has come true at last.' And now that I have written *that* down, I am not sure that my father told Jock. My brother could have known, without being told, of something that was so important to me, just as I could pick out of the air what was important to him.

I remember that when he read *My Friends the Hungry Generation*, he asked me: 'How did you come by that bit about the sinking of the Bismarck?'

I said: 'Did it ring true?'

'It *was* true,' he told me. 'You put into words what I felt and have never been able to say.'

My next question sounded odd even as I asked it: '*Were* you at the sinking of the Bismarck?' for the question came out of the gulf between telepathic knowledge and factual knowledge.

'Yes,' Jock said, 'and that was how I felt and why I never speak of it.'

My relationship with Sandy was deep but in the nature of things quite different. There are so many faces of what we call 'love' and being more percipient and precise than we are, the Greeks had not 'a' but four words for it. I had few reserves from Sandy but I did not tell him of my desire to write. The primary reason for this may have been the long habit of secrecy but I think there was another factor. I think I had the idea that, like my father, Sandy would think I was cherishing an unattainable dream and that this disbelief of his in my ability would weaken further the already faint spark that remained in me. Ten years of war, difficult peace and the forming of a strange new relationship which brought in its train a journey to a new world had intervened since I had tried to write anything so that, when we moved to the sugar plantation and I became a housewife with time on my hands, I lapsed into my old vice of writing in secret. If we had had children, matters might have been different but there is no 'if' in the weather of the world. The wind bloweth where it listeth and our natures respond to its drift in whatever way they can.

In 1953, Sandy's heart disease was diagnosed and discovered to be of long standing and from then on illness brooded over our home as the vultures brooded on the trees around it. Sandy was not at this stage incapacitated, was still working but the anxiety about over-strain was constant. I escaped, I suppose, when all my household and dietary duties had been completed, into writing. Then there came the time when I knew that not only illness was with us but also that death was not far away. It was then that I made my desperate throw and wrote to the literary agents in London.

When *My Friend Muriel* was accepted, I told Sandy what I had done. He was very weak and ill but first his face showed amazement, almost inability to believe what I had said and then came the words: 'Maybe you are going to *need* to be a writer. I am—' but I stopped him from saying it. I could not bear the words 'die' or 'death'. The contract for *My Friend Muriel* arrived on my birthday, the tenth of March, as I have said. Sandy read it and on the twenty-second of March at eleven-thirty at night I had to face not only the word 'death' but the fact that Sandy was dead.

Then came the months in the 'ideal haven', the entry in London into the strange new world of writing, then the return to George and my 'place' and the discovery of those four new members of the Cameron family. It was like being born anew into a strange world and I felt, looking at the children, like Shakespeare's Miranda when she said: 'Oh brave new world, that has such people in't.'

After that first Easter holiday with the children at the cottage, it was obvious that they were not going to grow any smaller so I thought that the cottage must be made bigger but the architect I consulted pointed out that an addition of the size needed, stuck on the back, would reduce the garden as well as spoiling the village character of the cottage. He pointed to this barn on the shore at the end of the cottage garden, asked if I owned it and when I told him I did not, he went away.

The barn belonged, although it took a few days for this fact to emerge from the depths of my slow-moving mind, to George's brother-in-law, known, as is common here, by the name of his farm, as Johnnie Ardoch. (This farm was once part of Poyntzfield estate and retains the old name.)

'Do you think Johnnie Ardoch would sell the old store?' I asked George.

This rectangular block of rough whinstone masonry was built in the 1830s as a co-operative store for potatoes on the ground floor and oats in the granary above. The high tide of the Cromarty Firth comes to within four yards of its north wall and the low tide exposes a flat beach of stones, clay and sand of about a mile in extent from north wall to water's edge. George could remember when the little cargo ship used to come in on the tide and allow it to go out, beaching her, whereupon the horses and carts, laden with grain and potatoes, would go out and load her, taking off for their return trip the goods that she had brought. George told me that the horses used to be wading up to their bellies on their first trip out for the captain, anxious to make a quick turn-round, presented the first man to reach the boat with a big dram of whisky.

It was from this yarn of George's that I developed the coal boat scene in *My Friends the Miss Boyds*. I do not think that any destroyer steamed into the Firth, blowing her siren, on Armistice Day in 1918, although I met a woman a few years ago who said that she remembered the scene 'as if it was yesterday'. Nobody else in the district remembers the destroyer and if she did steam in, I was not here to see her. On Armistice Day in 1918, I was at Balloch, Dunbartonshire and the scene I saw was much more like the Armistice Day described in *Jean in the Morning*. Jock, my brother, was born at Balloch in 1920.

When I asked George if Johnnie Ardoch would sell the old store, his reply was: 'One can only ask him and I'll take a walk up to Ardoch on Sunday,' but by the time Sunday came, I had little hope, for I had learned by now that Johnnie had refused several offers for the old building. I even began to toy with the idea of trying to buy back The Colony, only the buildings and enough ground for a garden, but it was rather a 'down to Wick' project for there were neither electricity nor telephone cables within a mile of it and I had to have both. But George took his walk up to Ardoch on the Sunday and Johnnie said: 'Ach, surely, George, the lassie can get the old store.' I bought the building in May of 1960 and the work of conversion began at once but it was March of 1962 before George and I could move in.

The Cameron family came to the cottage for the Christmas holidays of 1961, the children in better fighting form than ever, what with the cold and general bad weather out-of-doors. Their equivalent of the clansmen's battle-cry of 'Christ and no quarter!' was 'It's not fair!' 'It's not fair! His orange is bigger than mine!' and one evening the cry from the three older ones was: 'It's not fair, Auntie Bet! You keep on writing books for Mummy and Daddy to read and none for us!' I replied that I did not write books for them because I did not know what sort of stories they liked, unless they were stories about people who did nothing but fight all the time, but early in January of 1962, my brother sent me three-quarters of a page of foolscap typed in single spacing which 'shows you the kind of story us Camerons like'. Jock had typed out the children's concoction verbatim.

I once heard Geoffrey Trease, the well-known writer for children, speak about his work to this effect: 'The first thing in a story for children is somehow to get rid of all the Mums, for when you are just about to climb down the cliff after the pirates, Mum would say: No, no, it's too dangerous!'

No words were ever more true. The Camerons' story began with a longish factual paragraph about being on holiday, then leaving for home in the car with Father, Mother and the baby but when the second paragraph opened, Mother, Father and the baby had mysteriously disappeared without a word to mark their passing and the three Camerons were on a train and there were *robbers* on the train and everything ended up with the Camerons pulling the communication cord and the robbers getting caught.

My niece and nephews had been on a train very seldom at this time. Like many children of their generation, they had been taken nearly everywhere by car and in 1962, up here in the Highlands, we still had the old, impressive puffing steam trains on the minor lines.

Indeed, on my files, I find a copy of a letter dated 10 September, 1960 in which I am writing to my publishers to tell them of my safe arrival home from a trip to London and from it I quote: '– journey home from Perth to Inverness, hauled by two of these new diesel engines with the coy contralto voices which sound very silly among the Grampians.' And Perth to Inverness is the main Highland line.

The genesis of the Camerons' story was their desire to travel on a train, pull the communication cord and not have to pay the five-pound penalty for misuse, so I clothed their desire in words and called the result *Camerons on the Train*. When I typed the script, I typed two copies, sending one to the children and one to my editor on the fifteenth of February, 1962. By the third of April, the book was going into print.

By this time, little Iain who had been born in the spring of 1958 was four years old and had become the most important member of our family. This had come about by my brother's handling of the difficulty of integrating a Mongol child into the lives of three older children who were, academically speaking, all on the bright side. I do not know how he set about it but he achieved his end and at last Betty, who suffered from a quite illogical yet insurmountable guilt complex about Iain's condition, almost to the point of total nervous breakdown, came back to normal. Where the other three children were concerned, I think Jock contrived the integration by example and straight answers to straight questions. 'Iain does not talk yet because his brain is different from yours,' he would tell them and then turn to Iain: 'You are the very best boy in all Jemimaville, aren't you?' Iain, at that time, did not understand words but like all children and especially Mongol children, he recognised love, responded to it and now, at sixteen years old, he is still the most loving and lovable member of the family.

After *Camerons on the Train*, the children were asking for another book, so I wrote *Camerons on the Hills* but it was Iain's conquest of the family that lay behind *Camerons at the Castle* which is my own favourite of all the books I have written. I have said that I never look at my books again after they are accepted for publication. I was speaking of the novels, not of *Camerons at the Castle*. Every adult knows that no diamond crucifix has been found in a Highland castle during the last few years but many people who know us as a family know what enrichment Iain the Changeling has brought to us.

Before I sent the typescript of *Camerons at the Castle* to London, I sent it to my brother, telling him that I would not offer it for publication without his permission. He telephoned me on the evening of the day he received the script and said: 'This is an extraordinary document and I think it ought to be published. I think it may bring comfort to a great many parents.' I had not thought of the book in this light and, diffident as always, said that the Children's Books editor at Macmillan might not accept it at all but Jock was right on both counts. He sent the script direct to London in October of 1963 and it was accepted by the Children's Books editor in these words: 'I have just read *Camerons at the Castle* and think it is absolutely wonderful,' but it was much more pleasing than this to hear, later, from many parents of handicapped children that the book had brought them pleasure and comfort.

As I write this letter, I keep making little discoveries about myself and the members of my family and buried memories keep coming up from the past and now the memory comes to me of the only, I think, near-to-close friend of something like my own age that I made as a child. He was a handicapped boy. He came into my life when I was eleven years old, when my father was stationed at Croy, in what was then a whinstone-quarrying and coalmining district of Dunbartonshire. This is the background from which *My Friends from Cairnton* sprang and Tom was like myself, the policeman's child, something of an outcast. I never visited Tom's home but I have an idea that he was outcast because he was an illegitimate child. He was not a Mongol, like my nephew Iain, but a neglected child of the type that nowadays would be categorised as a 'slow learner'. By the time I met him, Tom had acquired little academic learning but, probably through necessity in his harsh circumstances, he had acquired the cunning necessary for survival.

We met only on Saturdays and in the evenings, for Tom did not attend my academy to which, from Croy, I went seven miles by train each day and we were friends for only the month of June, 1921. Croy was close to the Forth and Clyde Canal and also on the line of the Antonine Wall and now I remember that when Tom was not available for company, I spent my time in a stretch of the overgrown fossa in the company of an imaginary Roman legionary called Julius. I had begun to learn Latin at school and used to greet him properly, my right hand raised: 'Ave, Julius!' when he appeared on the grey boulder under the rowan tree in his splendid helmet and with his tall spear in his hand but from then on the conversation was in English until the moment of parting: 'Vale, Julius.' Julius was very real to me and I learned quite a lot about Italy from him, because he listened while I told him about The Colony and it was mere politeness on my part to show an interest in *his* country by reading about it anywhere I could.

My mother was dead now and we had a housekeeper – not Kirsty, who came later – but a pleasant, efficient woman who very soon left us to be married and who, as was natural, had no great interest in me and was probably looking forward to having children of her own. In any case, I was accustomed to being on my own and my father did not worry about my roaming about in the fossa or up in the woods where the Roman Wall was or among the scrub and trees on the banks of the canal. I was an orderly, dependable child who always came home at my bed-time and seldom got into mischief except with George and now with Tom, but my father did not know about Tom as yet.

Tom's and my haunt was the bank of the canal along which, in those days, slow horses pulled barges full of scrap iron going one way and barges full of pig iron going the other and there was *The Gypsy Queen*, a pleasure boat with engines and paddles, rather like a scaled-down model of the famous Mississippi paddle steamers, which sailed eastwards in the afternoons and west-wards in the evenings. There was some sort of mechanical organ aboard her which made a raucous noise like a merry-go-round and the passengers danced and sang rowdily as they sailed along, throwing their empty bottles out on to the bank. It was Tom who taught me that whisky bottles were of no use but that some bottles could be traded for toffee at the shop beside the canal bridge.

It was on the canal bank that Tom and I originally met. All sorts of jetsam floated on the water and on the day I met Tom I had found one of those wooden sectioned boxes which held a dozen large bottles of lemonade. I had attached a floating piece of rope to one of its rope handles, had filled the sections with sprays of hawthorn and young beech leaves and was pulling it along as a floating island. I had heard, by this time, the Legend of Loch Lomond which was reputed to have a fish without a fin, a wave without a wind and a floating island.

Tom spoke to me, explained that my find was worth a shilling and I thanked him for the information and said that we would go 'halvers' but Tom had a better idea. We would hide the box among the scrub, find a dozen bottles to fill it, then take the lot to the shop and have a real beano. With two shillings, he said, we could even have some Best Treacle Caramels.

For the remainder of the month, we searched diligently on Saturdays and in the evenings and by the last Saturday of the month we had the full complement of bottles in the box, which we carried between us, a rope handle each, to the shop at the bridge. On the way, Tom explained to me that I would go alone into the shop with the booty. 'She cheats me, the auld bitch,' he said. 'She'd only gi'e one an' six but she'll be feared to cheat the polisman's lassie.' He now handed me a large paper bag to hold our sweets and I staggered into the shop with the box. Under the grudging eyes of the mean, cross old woman, I put bars of toffee and chocolate into the bag and finally made her weigh out a pound of Best Treacle Caramels and left the shop with the huge bag of sweets but as I came out through the door under its ringing bell, Tom stuck his moon face in and shouted: 'Got ye this time, ye auld bitch! There's nae erses in they bottles!' whereupon he and I ran for our lives away along the canal bank to the shelter of the scrub. Over the blissful picnic of sweets, the Best Treacle Caramels being kept for last, Tom told me that at times when I had not been present, he had knocked the bottom out of every bottle with a stone and we rolled about on the grass in an ecstasy of glee.

That evening, however, near my bedtime, the shop woman came to the police station and reported us. In this Croy station, a door led direct from our living-room to the office and our housekeeper's eyes grew round and mine rounder with terror as we listened to the high-pitched tirade. 'Ca' yersel' a polisman an' yer lassie's jist a common thief! They'll go tae the clink, that's what they will!'

Then my father called me through to the office. I was shaking with fright but when he looked down at me he was not wearing his policeman's face. I learned later that, although my father was never ambitious enough to attain high rank, he was much respected in the force for his ability to assess the people of his district and keep the peace in it. He knew that this woman was notorious for cheating children and giving short weight in sugar and other commodities to the hard-pressed miners' wives who, encumbered with young children, could not walk the mile or so to the next shop.

'You tell me your side of the story,' my father said to me and I did, explaining that I did not know of the condition of the bottles and then he turned to the woman on the other side of the heavy mahogany office bar. 'You have no case at law, Mistress,' he told her. 'You should have examined the bottles before you accepted them. You just made a bad bargain of your own free will.' The woman screamed and stamped and cursed but to no avail. My father raised the flap in the bar, went through and opened the outer door. 'You know, Mistress,' he said now, 'if you cheat people, you must expect to be cheated. That is the way of the world,' and the woman went away without another word.

I went off to The Colony a few days later and Croy and Tom with it went out of my mind. I never saw Tom again but since my Mongol nephew was born and the question as to why children should be born handicapped has been raised, my only reply has been the illogical one that it is my belief that every human being, handicapped or not, has some contribution to make. Perhaps my holding of this belief is not so illogical after all, for it was through Tom, the outcast, that I came to know that 'If you cheat people, you must expect to be cheated'. This was Tom's contribution to me and I am sure he has, by this time, made many more contributions to many more people. I should think he is a business tycoon by now for, 'backward' as he was supposed to be, he had an instinctive knowledge of 'the way of the world' and of how to sway that way to his own benefit.

I like to write books for children and about children because I like children and remember what it was like to be a child. I remember the sense of utter and unjust defeat by the total lack of logic of the adult world.

The housewives of my family were proud of their craft, as they had a right to be, for my grandmother had introduced time and motion methods at The Colony before this science was recognised, before Messrs Lyons of Corner House fame, on the advice of time and motion experts, introduced one door for entrance from restaurant to kitchen and a second door for entrance to restaurant from kitchen. No unproductive steps were allowed in the management of The Colony household. There was a number of chores that were done every day, like the feeding of the household and the animals but each day had its special additional task, such as the washing on Monday, the ironing on Tuesday, culminating in the 'weekend special baking' on Saturday anent the ease and idleness of Sunday. Every Saturday night, I had a bath in front of the kitchen fire and was supposed to wash my face and hands each morning of the week. Thinking of the household programme, I decided that some parts of me were being neglected, so I devised a programme whereby I washed feet and legs one day, neck and arms the next and so on until the morning came when my grandmother asked suspiciously: 'Did you wash your face this morning?'

'No, Granny,' I said. 'It isn't my day for it.'

'Don't you dare give me a back answer, you impertinent little girl!' was her response. Few adults, except George, made any sense.

And I also remember the terror of those moments when the shop woman said I must go to gaol and I remember the bliss of those Best Treacle Caramels, eaten with Tom on the grassy bank of the canal, while *The Gypsy Queen* sailed by, her mechanical organ blaring:

> *There's a long long trail a-winding*
> *To the land of my dreams—*

Chapter 12

What sort of books do you read and have you any hobbies?
All sorts of books and as many as I have time to read. I do not
think I have any hobbies.

Since I began to write full-time for my living, my reading has
of necessity been curtailed. Newspapers were the first to go and
I receive my news nowadays from radio in the early morning
and from television in the evening, if I am not writing and
remember to switch it on. I read few modern novels, only those
which cause a big furore, such as Boris Pasternak's *Doctor
Zhivago* or *The Leopard* by Giuseppe di Lampedusa. Gone are
the university days when I was avid for the latest novel to leave
the printing press. My favourite reading now is philosophy,
biography and letters, especially those of writers, the classic
novels in English and the classic novels in other languages in
translation and finally serious works of literary criticism.

I once heard a man say: 'I never read the same book twice,'
and along with the man who once said to me: 'I never read books
by women,' I put him down in my mind as illiterate. In my view,
the English-speaking person who has not read *Middlemarch* by
George Eliot is simply not literate in his or her language and
Mary Ann Evans was no doubt aware of the existence of men
who did not read the work of women when she chose the
pseudonym 'George Eliot'. Writers do give readers every chance
they can to achieve literacy.

For the 'I never read the same book twice' man, I can do no
better than refer him to the final sentences of an article by the
poet, critic and novelist, John Wain, collected in a volume of
essays, *A House for the Truth* (1972). It is entitled 'The Meaning
of "Doctor Zhivago"' and the final sentences read: 'To appre-
hend and assimilate a great work of literature is a corporate
undertaking. Everybody adds his bit and this is mine.' By reading a good book twice or ten times one adds one's own new
'bit' to one's apprehension and assimilation with each new reading.

I have found that many people confuse the art of criticism with the craft of reviewing as practised in the columns of the newspapers and periodicals. The two have very little in common and the effect on the writer who reads criticism and reviews, I find, is that in the main criticism is helpful and constructive, reviews in the main unhelpful and destructive if one allows them to be so.

The professional reviewer must be the apotheosis of the man who 'never reads the same book twice' for the valid reason that he cannot have the time. To make a living by reviewing, I should think it would be necessary to read at least ten books a week in addition to writing the reviews themselves, while if reviewing is done as a side-line by what George once called 'a stickit novelist', it is bound to be at best a half-hearted and half-headed affair.

My own reviewing has been restricted to two attempts which I made on request. The first was an attempt on what I thought was a well-written novel on an interesting subject and period and I said what I thought but, although my review was published, I have never had another request from that quarter. I think that what I wrote was not bitchy enough to make popular reading. The second was for a reprint of *A Scots Quair* by Lewis Grassic Gibbon and in its published form my review had been so edited that the main point I had been trying to make had disappeared, so I no longer undertake this kind of work.

My publishers send me, I should think, about ninety per cent of all the reviews of my own work that are published throughout the English-speaking world and I read every one of them but, as in the Arab proverb 'the dogs bark, but the caravan moves on' I just go on writing, irritatingly to reviewers no doubt, unmoved by praise or execration. The readers who matter to me are not those who read for a few pounds a novel but those who read for pleasure and interest, for escape into another world.

'Escapism' is one of those words which, when applied to reading, has taken on a derogatory meaning, but all reading of poetry, stories, all going to the theatre, all attention paid to any of the arts is an attempt to escape from the self, from the trivia of every day into a world of new meanings and different experiences and if we are lucky and the writer is good enough, we may bring back from that world some newnesses and differences of thought that will colour and expand our own world of every day.

In an earlier chapter, I said that I would never denigrate the work of any honest writer, by which I mean any writer who is trying to record on paper the truth as he sees it. I have been accused in reviews, from time to time, of being a Pollyanna for whom everything in life turns out happily, of not being what is called 'realistic'. Some years ago, at a press conference in London, a young reporter who gave me the impression that he had never read anything that I had written but nonetheless despised all that I had written, said there was 'none of the real meat of life, well, sex and so on, in my books, was there?' I replied that I assumed a modicum of intelligence in my readers so that when I wrote that two people were married or were lovers, I expected the reader to know what this implied. I am afraid I added, also, that if the young man did not know what marriage implied, he ought to go home and ask his mother.

I try to deal honestly with sexual matters insofar as they affect the story I am telling, as in *My Friend Cousin Emmie*, but I think that a detailed description of any act of sex is doomed to failure from the start. A sexual act, to be meaningful to those engaged in it, must be private and that particular act can never have real meaning for anyone else. In the act of attempting to describe it, the privacy is destroyed and with it the meaning, so why give words and paper to the meaningless? I see this matter as simply as this.

Words are a product of the mind first and are spoken through the mouth or written through the point of a pen second but the language we have developed is, as yet, too limited to describe an activity in which both mind and body are engaged without getting the description out of balance. In the case of sex, it is only too easy for the balance to tip in the direction of the pornographic.

A writer can write only out of his experience and his experience is limited by the capacity of his mind to absorb what the course of his physical life has laid before him. I have given you here a few facts about the course of my life and the books I have written are the expanded construction which my mind has made on the basis of those and all the other facts of my life.

My life has not contained what the young reporter would

have called 'meaty' people and experiences. It has been, as you will have gathered, an 'ordinary' life, as we say, forgetting as we do that no life is ordinary but that all are extraordinary in their individuality. If the characters in my novels are too good, too kind, too 'nice' as some reviewers have implied, this is because I have been lucky enough to encounter, in the main, good, kind and 'nice' people on my way through life. There was nothing 'nasty in the woodshed' at The Colony, only the wood, old Tibbie the grey cat and her kittens in the box in the corner and the latest bundle of books, bought by George for a few pence at some auction sale, which I had to dust before my grandmother would allow them to come into the house.

An idea has been abroad for a long time that Tragedy is the highest form of literature and the only form worth aiming at but I do not agree with this and I am glad to read that Aldous Huxley, too, does not agree. It may be that I disagree with the idea because I could never write tragedy for I am, I think, an incurable optimist with a passionate conviction that life is good and that we must stress the good in it, not the pain. I doubt the tragic concept of 'purging by pity and terror'.

In sixty-four years, I have loved many people and have now lost most of them to death but, of peasant blood as I am, I accept that as I accept the turn of the seasons from spring through to winter. It was good to have known them and to have loved them and the love itself does not die but lives on in memory.

I could not be other than an optimist for I was taught early, by George, to put the sadness behind and turn to the forward-looking side. Those bundles of books which he bought at auction sales were, to me, bundles of mystery for you never knew what might come to light when you untied the string and examined the books one by one. The bundle might have come from some manse, following the death of some old learned divine, it might have come from some farmhouse that was changing hands or it might have been sent into the auction rooms by some housewife who was tired of dusting some bookish son's 'rubbish'. Kirsty disposed of most of the books I had collected since childhood as 'rubbish' by giving them to paper salvage campaigns during the war.

George and I acquired everything from volumes of sermons to the works of Conan Doyle, bound volumes of agricultural reports to *The Wide Wide World*, a complete set of the Waverley Novels, Palgrave's *Golden Treasury* and a volume of nonsense poems by Edward Lear. Our library was stored partly in our bedrooms, to be handy for Sunday reading and partly in the granary, to be handy for illicit reading during the week. 'I am fair scundered with this job,' George would say to me in the barn on a wet day when we had been given some dull task such as mending grain sacks. 'What about a little o' the poetry?' and we would sneak along to the end of the steading and up the stair to the granary. I did the reading and neither of us understood half of what we read for, in *The Golden Treasury*, we would tackle anything from the sonnets of Shakespeare to Swinburne but we caught the rhythm of the verse and that was enough. When I read something like 'Lord Ullin's Daughter', however, and came to the last stanza:

> 'Twas vain; the loud waves lash'd the shore,
> Return or aid preventing;
> The waters wild went o'er his child,
> And he was left lamenting,

George would say: 'Ochee, ochone, that is terrible miserable! Where is the gentleman with the Jumblies?' and I would find the volume of Edward Lear in the row along by the wall and read to the end of *The Dong with a Luminous Nose*:

> This is the hour when forth he goes,
> 'The Dong with a luminous Nose!
> Yonder – over the plain he goes;
> He goes!
> He goes!
> The Dong with a luminous Nose!

'That's better,' George would say, 'than poor Lord Ullin's daughter.' He would knock out his pipe. 'The Dong gives me new heart to sew a few more o' these danged bags. Come on.'

'The Dong with a Luminous Nose' ended just as sadly as did 'Lord Ullin's Daughter' and it was only a long time later that I discovered that it gave George new heart because it is intrinsically a better poem, but the point I am trying to make is that George instilled in me very early the idea that life need not be all dull tasks like mending sacks, that you could always turn to the brighter side with 'a little o' the poetry', that there was no need to dwell on the drowning of Lord Ullin's daughter, that you could turn away and wander the Great Gromboolian Plain with the Dong with a Luminous Nose.

So now I have given you a few facts about my life and in his novel *Doctor Zhivago*, Boris Pasternak has this to say: '– facts don't exist until man puts into them something of his own, some measure of his own wilful, human genius – of fairy tale or myth.' Well, my books are the 'something of my own' into which I have put my facts.

And I shall tell you here, before they do, what some reviewers would write of that paragraph. They would write: 'Jane Duncan thinks she is on a level with Boris Pasternak. She could not be more mistaken.' But I am not mistaken. It would be the reviewer who misread me who would be mistaken. I know better than he does, probably, where I stand in relation to Boris Pasternak, for the odds are that I have read Pasternak more carefully than he has. This estimate of reviewers' attitudes is based on hard experience. In reply to a question about what books I read, once, I named Jane Austen and two minutes later I overheard the questioner tell a colleague: 'She seems to think she is a second Jane Austen.' It might be in order for the hangers-on of the writing world to 'watch their tongues'. Writers live by the process of watching and listening, after all and by remembering what they have seen and heard.

But let us give all men their due. Reviewers are at a disadvantage when they read a novel of mine, for the chance is that my name is unknown to them and they see what I regard as a chapter in the life of Janet Sandison or Jean Robertson – the novels *My Friends the Misses Kindness* or *Jean at Noon*, let us say – as one more novel complete in itself in the weekly bundle to be got through. I try to make each 'chapter' or novel complete in itself but maybe I did not succeed when a reviewer wrote: 'This writer has not complete control of her material.' But never mind. You who read the series in total assure me that I have my material fairly well within control.

Reading, as I do, most books that receive critical or even review acclaim, I occasionally come across one that I do not understand and therefore do not like. It is the most natural of reactions to dislike what we do not understand. But I would never say of such a work: 'This is a bad book.' What I do say is: 'This book is more than I can understand. It is probable therefore that its writer has a mental capacity greater than my own.'

I do not set myself up to be a critic, you see, because I regard criticism as a separate creative art form for which I have a great respect and for which I have not the capability. I can only pay tribute to some of the critics who have helped me, such as Cyril Connolly with his *Enemies of Promise*, Lionel Trilling, notably with his *The Liberal Imagination* and Edmund Wilson with his *Axel's Castle*. I cannot even describe the nature of the help, except to say that when a man thinks deeply and with love about any subject, his mind becomes creative, the creativity spills over into his written thought and some of that creativity is transferred to me as a reader through the written word.

Cyril Connolly describes the enemies of promise in a writer as the various weeds listed in a poem by George Crabbe. There are the 'nodding poppies' which Connolly sees as 'Day-dreams, conversation, drink and other narcotics', the 'slimy mallow' which he sees as 'popular success' and the 'charlock' which he sees as 'sex with its obsessions'. I have spoken of all these literary weeds and I now come to the non-literary weed in answer to the questions that are often asked about my hobbies.

My main relaxation, apart from reading, is gardening but it is more than a hobby, it is a sort of obsession. My garden is very small and I am not a good or clever gardener who grows a 'wonderful show' of flowers or who breeds new varieties. I merely have a passion for planting things and watching them grow and I derive equal pleasure from the development of a potato plant or a Super Star rose bush. My garden is a tangle of everything from fruit trees to alpines. Its best time is the spring, for I like the spring flowers best of all and find the first green spear of a daffodil showing through the earth far more beautiful than the showiest, grandest, largest bloom that can emerge from a King Alfred bulb.

In the cold spring of 1959, when I came home from the West Indies, when the March snow had melted, I looked out of the scullery window and saw a few little green shoots among the black earth of the long vegetable bed which George had deep-dug in November.

'What can that be in the vegetable plot?' I asked.

'That's some lilies that came in,' said George. 'They started with one bulb but there's quite a bunch now.'

'How did the bulb come in?'

'I don't know. With a load of dung, likely. But it came in and I didn't put it out. A lily or two does no harm.'

This is my attitude to my riot of a garden. Things come into it one way and another and I do not put many of them out. The children, when the barn was first converted, planted the first thing of all, a coniferous tree of a variety that I cannot name. It was six inches high when they planted it in a hole dug with a spoon from the kitchen and it is now about fifteen feet tall. If a seed of my Lady's Bedstraw takes root between two paving stones, I do not take it out but leave it to form its golden rods in the summer. If a wild rose decides to grow beside the plum tree, I leave it. A wild rose does no harm. But I do put out the nodding poppies, the slimy mallows, the charlocks and many other weeds and those that go out are the ones that George and I used to remove from the earth of The Colony. 'That Stinking Willie,' George used to say, referring to the ragwort, 'only grows on poor ground. We can't have its dirty yellow flowers telling the whole world that The Colony is poor ground,' but, as you must have realised, for me The Colony was and is the richest ground in the world.

The garden there was the province of the women of the family. George and my father were both good gardeners but this was not usual in a crofting and farming community. Certainly my grandfather would never have condescended to work in the garden, even as a young man and this attitude is in direct line from one of the earliest known civilisations, that of the nomadic tribe living in clearings in the forests. The garden, where wild plants found to be good nutritionally, medicinally or otherwise were domesticated was an extension of the cave or shelter and was tended by the women while the men went hunting or foraging.

So my interest in gardening began early, at some of my away homes with my father and at The Colony with George but it was my grandmother who dictated to us what vegetables were to be grown. At the north end, nearest to the house, there was a flower border with a syringa tree at one end which my grandmother called the 'lilyoak' of which, I believe, the word 'lilac' is a corruption. At the south end, there was a belt of rhubarb, a belt of gooseberries and a belt of blackcurrants, with a massive growth of very fragrant honeysuckle at their east ends. These beds were permanent and in the area in between the vegetables were grown.

My grandmother knew every quirk of the crofting economy, a closely intermeshed business in which nothing went to waste. A hen that had stopped laying was killed, the intestines given to the big sow, the rest eaten by us, the bones buried in the garden because they were not good for dogs or pigs and then the feathers were scalded in boiling water, dried and used to stuff mattresses and pillows. Rabbits were killed, the intestines except for the stomachs given to the big sow, the rest eaten by us, the bones buried in the garden, the skins dried and exchanged for bowls and kitchen utensils with the travelling tinkers and the stomachs went into a bowl and made rennet for the making of junket and cheese.

The garden, what with the bones and the manure from all sorts of animals and fowls, was a fertile place and nothing that it produced was wasted either, not even the green caterpillars of the cabbage butterflies that tried to live in it. As soon as they appeared, a dozen little ducklings were turned into the garden and while the mother hen clucked anxiously outside the gate, they gorged themselves on the caterpillars. Their little feet did not trample the earth, their little beaks did not harm the young cabbages and when they had eaten every last caterpillar they slept for the rest of the day.

The family ate very well, I think but only a small portion of our food was bought in the Cromarty shops, only sugar (by the hundredweight except when war and rationing intervened), wheat flour, also by the hundredweight, the odd tin of corned beef, some fancy biscuits for the 'visitors' box', salt and a few other odds and ends. Tea came once a year from Edinburgh in a big silver-paper lined chest which, when empty, was excellent chicken-coop material; at weekends there would be several pounds of beef from the butcher to be boiled for the Sunday dinner and some bread and buns from the baker as a special treat. Our staple bread was the oatcake and scones made at home.

Twice a week, my friend Bella Beagle the fishwife tramped bare-footed up and over the hill with her creel on her back full of codlings, haddock and herring and once a year a barrel of salt herring was brought home and placed in a corner of the wood-shed, while trout and salmon could always be poached by George and me when the notion took us. Occasionally, too, if we had the time to spare, we would make an excursion down to Udale Bay behind this barn where I live now and at low tide, where the Gordons' Mills burn spreads crystal clear over the sand on its way to the salt sea, we would spear flounders a foot long with old table forks tied to sticks. There was considerable art in this and of course George was very proficient at it. You waded through the shallow water, slowly and carefully, until you felt the movement of the sand-buried flounder under your foot as the fish darted away, then you pounced with your spear. Being ticklish, I invariably fell flat on my back and speared very few fish, but it was a hot weather ploy and I was always dry again by the time we had climbed the hill back to The Colony.

Except for the commodities I have mentioned, we 'lived off the place'. George would not shoot more game than he could help but my grandfather and my father could both shoot and had less compunction. We had our own eggs, butter, milk, honey, cheese and jam made from garden and wild fruit. We had our own vegetables and above all our own oatmeal. A feature of both my homes was the meal barrel. At my away-home, it was a little one that held only half of that out-dated measure, the boll, which was one hundred and forty pounds, my dictionary tells me.

After harvest, when the first of The Colony oats was turned into meal at the mill at Rosemarkie, a half-boll was put on the train at Fortrose addressed to my away-home and at The Colony the meal barrel which stood in a corner of the kitchen was big enough to hold two bolls. At New Year, most of the two bolls put in after harvest would have been used, the barrel would have to be refilled during January and I remember one New Year when two of our guests had an argument which ended by one tipping the other head-first into the nearly empty meal barrel, so that only his heavy boots and part of his legs stuck out. My grandmother then scolded both guests very severely and sent them home.

We used very little coal but the coal we bought we really did use, including the ashes which filled ruts in the yard. In the main, our fires were of wood from trees cut on the moor by George and myself but we cut only trees whose appearance we disliked, such as those with twisted trunks or those that were storm-damaged. When my grandmother wanted to grill some slices of pork from a recently slaughtered pig, I would be sent to gather baskets of fallen fir cones which made a red, smokeless fire that yet imparted a delicious resinous flavour to the meat. I need not add that every ounce of the slaughtered pig was used in some way and some parts salted in a barrel that stood next to the salt herring barrel in the woodshed.

George and I did not ever cut down a tree without planting another. There were always plenty of little seedling trees growing among the heather too thickly for their own future health. It was my job to seek out suitable seedlings and when we had cut down the tree with our cross-cut saw and George had removed most of the roots from the ground with his axe and spade, he would say: 'Well, do you know of a tree that's just about your own age?' I would show him the chosen seedling, with his spade he would take out a great cube of the moor with the little tree standing in it and we would load it into the wheelbarrow and plant it in its new place, but only after we had poured a little fresh spring water from our tea-can and thrown a corner of our 'half-yoking' scones into the hole for luck.

'Half-yoking' is a word seldom heard even in these parts nowadays but the crofting day used to be divided into two yokings. The first began at five-thirty in the morning and George would feed the horses, then eat his own breakfast of porridge, tea, oatcake and scones and be ready to yoke the horses at six. My grandmother and the aunt-at-home would have been up at five to light the fire and by six they would be starting the milking. As a child, shadowing George, I worked the male programme. The first yoking ended at eleven and dinner was at eleven-thirty but the spell was broken at eight-thirty for half-yoking of tea and scones and jam which I fetched from house to place of work and George and I ate while the horses cropped some grass from the bank at the edge of the field. The second yoking began at one o'clock and ended at six, broken at three-thirty by the second half-yoking and by six-thirty we would have fed and groomed our horses and were now free to go into the house for supper.

The midday meal always consisted of soup, followed by meat or game or salt herring with potatoes and vegetables and then a milk pudding with cream and stewed fruit or jam, and supper started with porridge, followed by fish or home-cured ham or eggs and then tea, oatcakes, scones with butter, jam, honey. On Sundays there would be the baker's bread and buns and home-made fruit cake and shortbread.

I do not know what modern dieticians would think of our meals but it seems to me that they 'worked'. My grandfather died at ninety-six and my grandmother at eighty-four and they were never ill except for a day or two at the end of their lives. Of one thing I am convinced and that is that we of the 'advanced' countries today eat far too much and are led into far too many dietary fads. At the meals I have described, the helpings were small compared with the average helping served in a hotel nowadays. As a family we ate sparingly but the food was of good quality and fresh, completely free of chemical additives except for the last-ditch tin of corned beef. And never did I see a pill or a bottle of medicine at either of my homes. I suppose that it is because of this background that I feel sinful, while I have a garden, if I have to buy a potato and that I come out in an all-over rash if I take an aspirin to alleviate a head-ache brought on by too much reading.

When I came home from abroad and joined George at the cottage, he used to chuckle over our eight-thirty breakfast: 'If Herself could see us now, lying in bed till half-yoking!' and sometimes, even now, on dark, winter mornings, I think I see her tall, outraged figure in the shadows as I come downstairs and hear her stern voice: 'It's long past six of the clock! If you don't sow, you'll never reap.'

The answer to the questions that head this chapter are that I read as much as I have time to read and I garden obsessively because the need to do it was born in me, but I have no hobbies. My grandmother did not hold with hobbies or dilettanteism of any kind. 'Either do the thing or don't do it,' she used to say, 'but don't fiddle about with it!' So reading and gardening are things I do. I also do a little writing in between times in the way that my grandmother used to accuse George and me of 'capering about the day long and doing a little work in between times', but capering about or not, the work of The Colony got done, despite years of capering about, these books of mine have got written, and this long letter is nearly completely written too.

Chapter 13

Vale, Julius!

A life that extends over sixty-four years is almost certain to contain a few permanent goodbyes, but they are permanent only in a physical sense. All the people I have loved live on for me in memory and hardly a day passes that I am not reminded of them by something in the house or the garden, by something I read or by a swathe of mist along the hills.

'Mist on the hill is water for the mill, And mist on the sea is honey for the bee,' George used to say and 'Do the best you can. Nobody can do more,' my father used to tell me and this comes to mind with everything I try to do, be it dishwashing or writing a novel.

I hope that by having written so much about all these people I loved, I have not given the impression of nostalgic hankering after the dead past. I know that the only true way is forward and it is forward that I should like to go but I cannot but think that I am a lesser person than those forebears of mine. I am always aware that they lived on a hilltop, closer to the bright blue sky than this house on the shore where I live now. I have returned, if you like, to the meeting-place of sea and land where human life first began, have descended from their higher place to the bottom of the scale.

Those people had a closer kinship with the nourishing earth than we have nowadays and they had a respect for the world of nature around them that we seem to be losing. They co-operated with the elements while we speak of 'conquering' them and they walked the earth with humility instead of arrogance. I think it possible that we have something to learn from such people. We cannot go back in time but we can try to bring some of their attitudes forward and incorporate them into our own way of living. The race has always progressed by taking two steps forward and then one back and I think that, at the present time, we have taken far too many steps forward without a backward look and have overshot our little selves, but there is still hope.

Jesus Christ was born when the known world of two thousand years ago was collapsing into chaos and although I cannot visualise a new Messiah for our present collapsing world, I believe that, paradoxically, our own sin of self-love will stop us destroying ourselves. I think it will be a long time before we reach the pinnacle of loving one another as we love ourselves, as Christ commanded us to do, but maybe we can learn, even as we scramble to preserve our primitive selves on this shoreline between the known past and the unknown future, that hate is a bad word, that hate is something we can do and something that destroys ourselves as well as those we try to destroy.

There was always a sad moment at twilight when I had to part with my Roman legionary, Julius. He used to fade away into the shadows of the fossa and I used to walk home to bed, wondering if I had encountered the spirit of a real Roman soldier who had died on the Antonine Wall long ago. There was always the conviction that 'something' had been 'there' on that grey boulder under the rowan tree and I still have the conviction about the people I have loved that something of them is still here.

By the time I became friends with Julius, I had already said goodbye to my baby sister and my mother and in 1934 I said goodbye to my grandparents. In 1951, I had to say it at long distance from the West Indies to my father, then in 1956, I had to say it to Sandy.

I am now reminded of a minor question that has often been asked and which I have not answered in this letter. 'How did you arrive,' people often ask, 'at Alexander Alexander as a name and Twice as a nickname?' I took Sandy's real forename for my fictional character, which is only a little bit of the real man and then by that queer process of fictionalising which I cannot explain, a fact arose out of my memory. At Renton, when I was not more than three – I know this because Catherine arrived a month after my fourth birthday and she had not yet been born – I made the discovery that people had all sorts of different names. I became obsessed with names, questioned the grocer, the butcher, the postman: 'Tell me your name, please,' to the embarrassment of my mother who failed to stop the questions but made me add the 'please'. One of those

148

I questioned was a colleague of my father who came from the Isle of Skye and spoke in the soft voice of that island with its richness of vowels.

'Dougal MacDougal,' he replied.

I remember my pleasure in the most unusual name I had heard so far. 'Dougal and Dougal *again?*'

'Yes. Twice Dougal.'

There was the name I wanted for my fictional character. Alexander Alexander. Twice Alexander.

Constable Dougal MacDougal had a generous attitude to spelling of which I learned later and which I have always admired. In one of his weekly reports, he wrote of 'mischievious and mallicious dammage' and when my father pointed out that the phrase contained an 'i', an 'l' and an 'm' too many, he said: 'But you understand what I am writing?' My father agreed that he understood and Dougal then said: 'As long as you are understanding, a few extra letters is neither here nor there.' Dougal, it seems to me, had grasped the basic principle of language, written or spoken, that understanding between writer or speaker and reader or listener was the important thing.

I am not, I hope, a hypocrite, at least not enough of a hypocrite to say that it was hard to part with Old Kirsty. In that spring of 1959, when George's lilies flowered in the middle of the vegetable plot, life showed its ironic side. Old Kirsty, who had left the cottage the year before to stay with relations, had moved around them all, quarrelling with them all until at last she fetched up in lodgings. There, she suffered a stroke which rendered her unconscious and she was taken to hospital. Nobody knew anything about her, who she was other than that her name was Mrs Cameron. There was nothing to indicate that she had any relatives but a chance visitor to the ward recognised her as the Mrs Cameron who used to live at Rose Cottage, Jemimaville. I was told of this and telephoned the hospital to be informed that she had died and the nursing sister's relief that her 'relatives' had been traced was palpable. And so George, Jock and I, the people whom Old Kirsty had most disliked, were the people who rescued her from a probably unknown grave.

The next to go was Grandpa who outlived his son by six years, and Jean has gone too, but I think you will understand that the saddest loss of all for me since the death of Sandy was the loss of George.

On the nineteenth of March, 1968, he died during the afternoon, here in this house which was his home, the place, I think, where we should all like to die, instead of in the white anonymity of a hospital. In January of 1966, at the age of eighty-seven, he suffered a stroke which paralysed his left arm and leg but brought no paralysis to his mind or spirit. With the help of some of our neighbours, we moved his bed and my own down from our bedrooms to the large ground-floor living-room so that I was with him, day and night, for two years and two months, except for two two-week periods when Jock, Betty and the children took charge while I went to London to see my publishers. Iain, at these times, elected himself head nurse, directing my brother in helping George from his bed to his chair by the fire, then tucking the knee-rug in with his fat, gentle, solicitous little hands. Iain could now speak a few words and George would say: 'Tell me now, Iain, were you ever down at Wick?' and Iain who can always recognise fun would reply: 'Yes, George!' and both would laugh uproariously. It was a happy two years until that early morning in March when I awoke with the feeling that something was very far wrong and found that George was not asleep but unconscious and he died that same afternoon.

At first, I felt his death as a great deprivation, felt that a great area of loving and caring had been taken out of my life, felt diminished and impoverished, but now this slight talent for writing came to my aid and I embarked on the Jean Robertson sequence, the first volume of which was published in 1969. After that sojourn in the ambience of what had been my away-home, I found that I could look round my real home, this barn here and I discovered that George, although he had gone from here, was still 'there' in a new dimension and that I could go on with the Reachfar series of novels, of which he is one of the main supports. It was now that I wrote one of the most difficult chapters, *My Friend the Swallow*, which records the death of Twice.

All these people who have died are still with me in memory and when I come in from the garden to my old atlas, my sheets of paper and my pen to do a little work, I feel as if I have left them out there for a little while. These people are part of me, any talent I have came from them, was developed by them and I was brought up by them to believe that bushels were for measuring oats, not for hiding talents. It may be said, perhaps, that I hid what talent I had for a long time but I think it was a slow-growing thing, like those trees that George and I used to plant on the moor at The Colony. All those people I knew were facts but I hope that, as Boris Pasternak said, I have put something of my own into what I have written of them so that, now, they have something of the quality of myth.

And now, before I end this letter, I must tell you of one more book that George brought home from an auction sale. I was about six at the time and had not even the slight knowledge of French that I had at the time I read about Daudet's rabbits. The book was by some Victorian gentleman and on its spine were the words: 'Belles Lettres by——Esquire.'

'Esquire,' George said, 'just fancy that. I have always thought a man should just call himself by his name and let others call him esquire if they want to. And I wonder why he should think that anybody would want to read his Belly's letters?'

I feel that what I have written here is a Belly letter and not a Belle Lettre but I wrote it because so many readers have asked: 'Are your books autobiographical?' This letter is fact and not fiction and you must all answer this question about my novels for yourselves.

Finally, I want to record my gratitude to all the people, which means everybody I have ever known, who helped me to become a writer and to all the people who have read, who read and who in future may read what I have written. I am deeply aware of and deeply grateful for my good fortune in realising a dream. It proves to me that, in spite of the weather of the world, dreams can be realised and that we all have the life-gift of the liberty to take a notion and go down to Wick.

Yours sincerely,
JANE DUNCAN.

P.S. 'How long,' people ask, 'does it take to write a book?' Here is the schedule of this one. The first manuscript was written between 20 August and 8 September, 1974 and put into typescript between 9 and 15 September. When my editor and his colleagues read what I had written, their reaction was: 'Is there no more?' so I agreed to expand and revise the letter, which I did between 27 October and 24 November, 1974 on returning from London and a round of visits to friends. The final typescript was prepared between 25 November and 2 December, 1974. But I met Twice Dougal sixty-one years ago. How long, therefore, does it take to write a book?

J.D.